MW00893204

What others are saying...

"I believe that **Don't Wait, Dominate!** should be mandatory reading for anyone in the auto industry. Michael Cirillo has unselfishly shared his wisdom within the pages and anyone that reads it will be better for it."

- Tracy Myers C.M.D
Dealer Principal and Best-selling Author

"Michael Cirillo gets it. He sees around the curve and is telling dealers what they need to do to be ready for the future. I'd strongly recommend this book to anyone looking to embrace the future and do what it takes to dominate their industry!"

- Marcus Sheridan
The Sales Lion

"Michael Cirillo has turned the paradigm upside down. It's not about how to keep ahead of your competitors. With Cirillo's insights, dealers won't need to worry about having competition at all."

- JD Rucker
Founder of Dealer Authority

"In **Don't Wait, Dominate!** Michael provides the treasure map to dominating the web not just for auto dealers, but any business in today's noisy marketplace. This is a "textbook" disguised as a "book". "

- Robert Wiesman
Co-host of The Dealer Playbook Podcast

"Having success online doesn't have to be a pipe dream. Michael is clear and transparent while keeping you entertained. I can't recall the last time I had this much fun realizing all I didn't know about online marketing!"

- David R. Bradley
Sales and Marketing Manager, Grant Cardone Training

DON'T WAIT.
DOMINATE!

HOW TO RELEASE THE FLOODGATES OF OPPORTUNITY
FOR YOUR DEALERSHIP AND THRIVE ONLINE

MICHAEL A. CIRILLO

Don't Wait, DOMINATE! (Auto Dealer Edition)
How to Release the Floodgates of Opportunity for your
Dealership and THRIVE Online

Copyright

© 2014 by Michael A. Cirillo. All rights reserved.

Notice of Liability

Despite this book being about how to get more from your online marketing using a leveraged approach, it should be clearly understood that your success is not warrantied by you simply reading the book. All of the information presented here is provided "as is". We have taken every precaution in the preparation of this book, but neither Michael nor anyone else associated with the publication of this book shall be liable to any person or entity with respect to any loss or damage caused or alleged to be caused directly or indirectly by the information in this book. What you do with the strategies presented here is up to you. We hope you'll DOMINATE!

Notice of Rights

No part of this publication may be reproduced or transmitted in any form or by any means, electronic, mechanical, photocopying, recording, or otherwise, without the prior written permission of the publisher. For information on getting permission for reprints, excerpts and foreign translations, contact mc@michaelacirillo.com

Cirillo Marketing Group Inc.

www.MichaelACirillo.com

Credits

Book Design and Production: Colin Burke

Printed in the United States of America
ISBN-10: 1512179183
ISBN-13: 978-1512179187

First Edition

To my children, Dallin, Tristan and Aria. You are
the greatest accomplishment in my life.
And the women who God blessed me with,
the love of my life, Kara.

CONTENTS

INTRODUCTION
DON'T PROCRASTINATE GREATNESS

I had been in a management position
in my family business for 3 years when I
came to the conclusion that I wasn't
doing things the right way...

My company had so much competition in the market, and I was struggling to find ways to make an impact that would grow my business.

I felt like I was sinking to the bottom of the pack and needed to figure out a way to pull myself and my company out of obscurity. I was sick of having the best product that nobody had ever seen.

After thousands of hours of research and learning, I set out to try something that proved to be monumental for my company.

It was early 2012, and I was going to write an Ebook[1]about how to do automotive marketing the right way. The idea came to me after observing self-serving content with zero appeal. Dealers deserved (and still deserve) better.

There was only one problem.

I wasn't particularly that good at writing. My grammar sucked[2]. My ability to convey the right message through writing was minimal, at best.

But I had an idea, and it was simple.

I had been listening to dealers express concerns about shifting digital for years. I was going to provide them a roadmap in my eBook for how they could get started.

Zero sales pitch. Just good, actionable information that they could use no matter who their providers were.

I had many people tell me that I should think about enrolling in a creative writing course first. After all, you don't want to fail by writing an embarrassing book, right? Others expressed their concerns that I'd be shooting myself in the foot by providing too much information.

It wasn't a matter of preparation. I had become more than prepared. I had learned and practiced with the best minds in the marketing world, and I was ready to stop merely surviving and start thriving!

I sat down and began to write. From start to finish the entire eBook took only 12 hours to put together. I wrote the content, designed the cover art and put a process in place that would help maximize the effectiveness of the book.
And not just for those who read it. For my
company as well.

Looking back today at that eBook, I feel sheepish. My peers were right. I could have used a creative writing course and some grammar help.

But there is an
exception...

That single eBook has generated over **$250,000** in residual annual revenue to my business. Not bad for 12 hours of work that I did once several years ago, right?

I'm not telling you this to sound cocky or arrogant. I'm not telling you this to brag.

I share this with you because I know that by applying the right kind of marketing, you can see massive sustainable success, even at your dealership.

After I was successful in implementing the strategy for myself, I began to do it for others. In the time since, I've had the pleasure of working with thousands of small and medium businesses worldwide.

But we'll get into more detail about the specific strategies I've used throughout the rest of the book.

The point is that I took action and addressed the concerns and demand of the market. I provided something valuable, and it still resonates to this day for those looking for help.

I was one of very few "vendors" in the industry that focused on providing unbiased, relevant information that dealers could use regardless of whether they did business with me or not.

I stopped trying to be the same as every other website or "marketing expert" out there and began to follow a recipe that works.

If you want proof, take a close look at how self-serving the messaging is out there. It boggles my mind that people still think that providing little information will intrigue people to want to buy from them.

But this is what the "experts" are currently doing. We'll get more into this later on in the book...

How Does This Apply To You and Your Dealership?

At this very moment, you are sitting on an unlimited supply of high-quality vehicle shoppers.

There are millions of them, and they are prepared to hand over their hard earned money. That's right – they are ready to spend their money...but with who?

In the United States alone, new car sales topped $700[3] billion dollars in 2014. Consumers are opening their wallets and buying cars.

But if that's true, why are so many dealers (maybe you?) worried about how slow business has been since the economic downturn of '08?

Many of you are in the same boat that I was in. When I realized my problem, I needed to do something that separated me from the pack and pulled me out of obscurity.

At the end of the day, I produced information that brought me closer to the right shoppers who were prepared to do business with me. Sure, it was beyond valuable for them but it also served a purpose for me. There is nothing wrong with that. That should be the whole reason you're in business.

Serve the needs of your customers and increase profits (unless you're running a non-profit organization, that is).

There is a massive chasm separating you from vehicle shoppers. You may see, hear and even be near each other, but the gap between you and your buyers is still big enough to keep them from pouring into your store.

Okay, so I'm being a little dramatic with my analogy here.

The fact remains the same: things could definitely be better for your dealership, right? Why else would you be reading this book?

If so, you aren't **alone**.

Thousands of dealerships around the world are struggling to hit their targets. The web has changed the face of the auto industry. Dealerships that can't keep up suffer from slow traffic, poor quality leads and lost sales opportunities.

Every dealership acts, sounds and promote themselves the same way. How can you ever expect shoppers to pick you when they don't know what makes you unique?

You Should Be Doing Online Marketing, Shouldn't You?

I get asked this question all the time, often right when I begin working with my clients.

Some of them believe that online marketing means merely having a website. Others think that having listings on AutoTrader or similar sites is the magic bullet they've been looking for to help them battle the competition.

Others have dabbled in digital advertising or blogging

15

but have not realized any sustainable results.

By now, most dealers believe that they should be doing some level of online marketing, but don't know where or how to get started.

It's becoming increasingly difficult to know who to turn to for guidance. There are so many "experts" claiming that they have the secret to SEO success, web success or social media success.

They take to social media trying to solve the world's problems with controversial posts, attempting to get a rise out of those who may oppose their views. They think this behavior makes them look and sound smarter than their opponents, and in so doing portray them in the light of an expert. It doesn't.

But here is something that I've learned that you can take to the bank:

The proof of ability **is in results.**

My hope is that you will take the principles you learn from this book and put them to use. Don't be afraid to experiment. Find out ways to get the most out of what we're going to talk about here.

I know that what you discover here will give you more clarity about online marketing. I believe it because it has worked and continued to work for me. What we're going to look at in this book is filled with lessons I've learned that have brought my career in online marketing to a whole new level.

There is one caveat, though.

No, this isn't the fine print that accompanies other big claims you've heard. I only have one requirement from you as you become exposed to REAL online marketing…

There will be times (maybe even now) when you'll feel like you need to learn more before you get started.

I know that feeling very well.

You have to promise me that you'll push past that feeling and make your way on to execution. Execute on this information like your life depends on it.

Don't allow yourself to wait until you feel more prepared to take action, or you will likely never feel prepared enough to take action.

While others are busy assessing the risk of what it will take to be successful, you have a serious competitive advantage to do things today that they aren't willing to.

Don't procrastinate your greatness - let it shine.

Don't wait. DOMINATE!

Here we go…

DON'T WAIT, **DOMINATE!**

CREATE ONLINE SUCCESS
WITH THE THINGS YOU ALREADY HAVE

Believe it or not, everything you need to be successful online already exists.

To go a step further, you more than likely already have the tools and resources you need to get started.

To go one more step further, you're likely already using them.

So why aren't you getting the results you want? We'll get to that in a minute. But first...

A Brief Look Into My Childhood

I can remember being about nine years old when my dad called my siblings and me into his office. He had to show us this new thing called, "The Internet".

As we sat there anxiously waiting to connect to the internet through the phone line, I will never forget what my dad said to us.

> *"This is going to kill the encyclopedia salesman!"*

Back then I remember thinking, "Pfff, who would ever want to read the encyclopedia, anyway?" but talk about a prophecy!

The internet has changed the way we do business. Every industry on the planet has, in some way, shape or form become affected by the internet.

I completely understand that it may seem like the Internet

19

has complicated a perfectly good system of business, but there's a reason for that.

It has nothing to do with the Internet, though.

It has to do with those who are taking advantage of your lack of understanding. They are the reason that doing business online feels so difficult. They are the reason you're having a hard time knowing where or how to get started thriving, instead of merely surviving.

I see this all the time. After every conference, blog post, or webinar, dealers scramble the jets. Someone has just introduced them to a tool or piece of software that will solve all their problems.

Except for that, they don't. When will we catch on?

It's Not What You Have; It's How You're Using It

The internet, if anything, has added a layer of transparency to the consumer's path to purchase. It has empowered them to get the information they are looking for faster than ever.

On the flip side, it has enabled business owners to know more about potential buyers than ever before. Using the internet you can find out what interests the consumer, what topics are trending and even where to find and target them.

Prior to the internet, understanding the consumer's path to purchase was vague and unclear. There was much more guesswork, and the metrics that were available to us were from a single dimension.

Run ad, count store traffic, measure sales increases or decreases.

"Did you ask that customer how they found out about our sale today?"

"Oh crap, I forgot!"
"Well, just mark it down as 'the newspaper' then..."

Believe me when I tell you that the Internet isn't the issue. The issue isn't even that things appear to be more complicated or that they're moving too fast.

The real issue is that you don't yet know how to leverage the internet to get high returns.

Before I set out on my journey to learn as much as I could about online marketing, I was in the same boat.

I'd sit there for what felt like hours staring at a blank Google search page. I was desperate to type something – ANYTHING that would reveal how I could get more traffic, leads and sales.

I was doing everything I knew to be right. I had a website, and I was doing online advertising. I was trying to be active on social media. I even dabbled a little in creating videos.

Sound familiar?

I learned that just because you have a website or do PPC ads or even have a Facebook page - all of those things don't add up to online marketing.

How you treat those things **does.**

Back to what I was saying earlier. Everything that you need to thrive online already exists.

There is no new technology, software, marketing or advertising concept that you should be waiting for to become successful online.

And you know that piece of software that your web vendor has been hinting at developing? It's not going to serve as the magic bullet to more traffic, leads or sales either. Sorry.

Up to this point in my career I have had the pleasure of becoming associated with and learning from several successful online marketers.

I mean that they've built multi-million dollar empires using only the same tools that you have available to you right now.

Why am I telling you this?

I think it's important to understand how well equipped you are for success online. Whatever you don't have right now, you can get your hands on with a few clicks of the mouse. There are no new inventions that will take you to the next level.

I get that the internet may seem overwhelming. It may seem like everything is moving fast right now, but that's just because you're not up to speed yet.

But that's about to change for you - **forever!**

Here's What You'll Need to Succeed Online

We're going to look at each of these tools in more detail throughout the book, but for now, I just want to touch on them.

1. WEBSITE

I haven't run into this situation yet, but please make sure that you have a website. **It's 2015 for Pete's sake!**

With that, make sure that your website reflects the current calendar year. It's 2015 so do yourself a favor and make sure it looks current. In my observation, clothing designs are capable of recycling fashions from another era. We haven't quite reached that in web design.

A website that has the design and function of something created in 1999 won't work for you.

A website is also your main online property. It should act as the hub to all of your online marketing efforts.

2. EMAIL MARKETING

Email is still one of the most effective ways to market your business.

In fact, the most elite online marketers still rely deeply on email to connect with and sell to their audiences.

Of course, one of the most crucial elements of being able to market through email is having email recipients.

The beauty about this is that most dealerships have the equivalent of a small city worth of names in their CRMs that they can leverage. Those names represent thousands of people who have purchased or will purchase shortly.

That's a **goldmine!**

3. GOOGLE ANALYTICS/WEBMASTER TOOLS

Having access to Google Analytics and Webmaster tools is a powerful accountability mechanism. You need to be the owner of the data so that you can share access to your web vendors as needed.

Google analytics will help you make powerful strides toward success. When your habit is to make decisions based on what the data reveals, you become positioned for massive growth.

4. GOOGLE ADWORDS

Advertising is such a powerful element in the marketing mix.

Doing ads the right way, with the right targeting can generate instant traffic from targeted users.

Sadly, most dealers aren't doing online advertising the right way. As a result, the traffic is low quality, the cost is high and the return on investment is low.

5. SOCIAL NETWORKING/ADVERTISING

I get asked all the time if it's important to have a profile setup on every social network under the sun.

As crazy as this sounds, I actually don't recommend it.

In fact, I think it's flat out dumb.

It's one of those online myths that contribute to feeling overwhelmed and frustrated. After all, how could anyone keep up with consistently updating every social profile?

Each social network has its language. I believe that it's more important to focus on one or two social networks and focus on providing as much value as possible in that network's language.

New York Times Best-selling Author, Gary Vaynerchuk has written an awesome book all about this called, **"Jab, Jab, Jab, Right Hook".**

I recommend starting with Facebook since that's where everyone already is.

Again, more on how this fits in later...

6. VIDEO

Video creation is a must. But not just any video.

High-quality video.

High quality, engaging video.

Video creation is what my friend and co-host of The Dealer Playbook podcast, **Robert Wiesman** did to build a 6-figure income selling cars. He didn't even have to take fresh "ups" off the showroom floor as a result!

Another Car Pro, **Elise Kephart** used engaging follow up videos to set herself apart and achieve success in her market.

This day in age, videos are a must-have resource for anyone who wants to take their career or dealership to the next level of success.

The beauty is that you have what you need to make high-quality videos: a smartphone!

There you have it. Six tools you likely already have that will help you achieve massive online success.

Be honest, how many of the tools that I just listed don't you have access to? And the ones that you don't have, how easy would it be for you to get connected?

The point is if you want more traffic, leads and sales, you can leverage the tools you already own to harness the power of the internet.

We're going to look at each of these tools in more detail, but for now, let's talk about clutter…

CHAPTER ONE QUESTIONS

What are the six tools and resources that you already
have to help you succeed online?

What are some ways you can creatively use those tools
in your current online workflow?

DON'T WAIT, **DOMINATE!**

THE MARKET IS INCREDIBLY CLUTTERED
AND THAT'S YOUR MOST VALUABLE ASSET

It doesn't matter where you go these days; marketing will touch you in some way, shape or form. You can't escape it. It is a guarantee that by the time you go to bed tonight, marketing will have slipped its way into view.

The problem is that there is so much marketing going on around us all the time, that we've become conditioned to ignore it.

With over 20,000[4] franchise new car dealers in North America alone, the market is oversaturated. Consumers don't know who to trust or who to buy from.

Dealers are frantically trying to do whatever they can to take the spotlight. Often, that means they are spending more money than they need to on solutions that aren't necessarily working.

It's more difficult than ever for dealers to 'one up' the competition because everyone is saying the same thing.

But this is the perfect situation to be in, and I'll tell you why in a minute...

First, it's important to understand how the market got so

29

cluttered. Once you do, you will quickly learn how to use the clutter as your most valuable resource.

I recently had an interesting conversation with a 95-year-old women. These days, she spends most of her time doing crossword puzzles or crocheting blankets. But she is sharp as a tack and has a clear memory of the last 90 years!

As we were speaking, an interesting thought crossed my mind. She has lived through pretty much every cool invention that has shaped the world we now live.

I was curious and had to ask what she remembered seeing for the first time...

The jet engine, helicopters, the electric guitar and ballpoint pen. Not to mention all the advancements in medicine, engineering, frozen food and, of course, the world wide web in 1989[5]!

On top of that, she has seen the world get more cluttered with marketing.

Even though electricity had been around for a while, it hadn't reached mass distribution yet. Much of the country still lived by Rockefeller's kerosene or candle light after the sun went down.

But once electricity made it to where she lived, things changed forever.

With electricity came the radio. A new way to communicate and convey the value that was shortly followed by television. Each new piece of technology came with it a far greater ability to communicate. Advertisers took notice, and advantage!

As my Elderly friend reminisced about the good old days, she painted a mental picture that reminded me of, "Leave it To Beaver"...

Kids all washed up and in their pajamas. Dad was wearing his house blazer smoking a pipe with one hand and holding his favorite drink in the other. Mom was crocheting a blanket for one of the children, all together listening to their favorite after-dinner radio program.

Things were much different back then.

You could listen to a radio program without being bombarded with advertisements. Can we say the same today?

So how did everything get so cluttered?

There's nothing like a **swift smack upside the head**

Back in the day, the focus was on value.

True, each radio show included advertising. But they did the best they could to make it blend in as much as possible.

As radio and television audiences grew, so did the demand for more advertising. It was appealing for company's to leverage the massive audience to gain exposure for their products.

So the regular programming became shorter and shorter, and the ad space grew longer and longer.

It eventually became much more difficult to blend in the advertising. It quickly became disruptive. Like a swift smack upside the head.

The last time I checked, everyone I know hates being interrupted – especially when they're doing something they enjoy.
And we're still just talking about radio and tv here. What about magazines, movie pre-show commercials, billboards, posters, newspaper?

Heck, you can't even go to the bathroom in an airport anymore without having advertising in your face while you do your business!

But wait...there's more!

Notice how I haven't even mentioned the internet yet?

Take a minute to think about all the marketing that currently surrounds you, without the internet.

While that slowly sinks in, think about all the marketing that happens every minute of every day online.

Google Adwords, YouTube ads, Facebook ads, Twitter ads, LinkedIn ads, ads from phone apps. The list can keep going and going.

Where it starts to get redundant is when you click an ad to a website filled with ads! I feel like if the marketing and advertising loop enough we'll break the space-time continuum!

Better yet, how many people do you know that sit on the couch watching television with their laptop open and a smartphone in one hand? Three ways of viewing ads all at the same time!

Ok, so I was just describing myself there...but if I had to guess, I just described you too! And if I had to make another guess, I'd say that you (just like me) didn't notice any of the marketing or advertising.

Why not? Let me explain...

Do me a favor and open up the newspaper. Turn to the automotive advertising. What do you notice? Do all the ads look the same and use the same language? Is there anything that differentiates one ad from the next?

Or does each ad claim to have the lowest prices or best finance rates?

Is there anything compelling about the advertising that you're viewing? If not, it's safe to say that those ads are getting ignored.

Things are much more competitive now. It's common to see a Ford F-150 commercial followed by a Ram 1500 and shortly after that; a Toyota Tundra commercial.

It's not like back in the day where competing ads rarely played back to back.

At the top of the hour, Camel cigarettes owned the airwaves. At the bottom of the hour, Hoover vacuums.

Fast forward to today and how competitive everything is, and what does the consumer see and hear? I'll wrap it up for you in a nutshell...

*"Blah blah blah, Truck, **blah blah blah,** 0.9% blah financing..."*

If you're still reading this, chances are that this is the type of advertising you're doing. At this point, all I can tell you is that you're contributing to the clutter out there.

There is so much going on around us that we have shut it out.

But there is a way to cut through the clutter and use it to your ultimate advantage. Let's explore.

Marketing Quantity Multiplied by Crap, Still Equals Crap

I see this all the time. Dealers become debilitated because of all the motions that their competition is making with their marketing efforts.
They see all the newspaper ads and hear the radio spots. They begin to believe that their competitors website is better than their website or that they are getting better or more leads.

The fact is that if you've been focussing on any of the things I just mentioned, your focus is in the wrong place.

When you take a step back and look at the level of activity

out there between you and the competition, what I've been saying is true.

The market is cluttered.

It's cluttered with competing messages. It's cluttered with self-promotion. It's cluttered with price competition. It's cluttered with *"me, me, me"* and *"I, I, I"*!

It's cluttered with **CRAPPY Marketing.**

If you can wrap your head around how crappy the marketing out there is, the quantity of it no longer matters. The sum of a bunch of crappy marketing still equals crap, after all.

Just because your competition advertises "everywhere", or even if they have a bigger budget than you, that doesn't mean that what they're doing is good. Make sense?

Not only that, but if the market has become cluttered with crappy marketing, you have a competitive advantage. It means that great quality, impactful marketing is scarce. It means that there is a void in the marketplace that is just waiting to be filled.

How You Can Move the Needle in the Right Direction

One of the most appealing aspects of marketing online when the bar is so low is exactly that: the bar is SO low.

That means that you won't have to move the needle very far in the right direction to make a HUGE impact on your marketplace.

Think about it. Anything better than crap, will not just be great, it will be incredible!

Now don't get me wrong. I'm not saying that you should be lazy and only aim for being just a little better than everyone else.

I'm merely pointing out the fact that by starting to take any action in the direction of good marketing will create a gap between you and the competition.

A gap that they won't even begin to know how to bridge.

Our first instinct as human beings is to assume that just because someone is doing something a certain way, that they must know what they're doing.

I'm here to tell you that when it comes to online marketing, this couldn't be further from the truth, but it doesn't have to be.

It just is **right now.**

So how can you move the needle in the right direction? How can you take your career or store to the next level and rise above the clutter?

Stop paying attention to the competition!

The proof of ability is in results, and from what I've observed, the vast majority of dealerships are in survival mode.

The funny thing is that everyone is working so hard to outwit and outperform the competition, but everyone is doing the same thing.

Everyone is chasing one another. So if I'm chasing you, and you're chasing me and we're chasing them...who is the leader? See, if you spend your time paying attention to what the competition is doing, you will start to pattern your actions after them.

This behavior is counter-productive and won't help you with your online marketing.

You need to focus your energy on creating reasons why you're different, not the same. Your consumers NEED to know what makes you different and why they should trust you over your competitors.

Since you've likely been spending much of your time worrying about the competition and HOW to dominate, I'm hoping you've noticed the one BIG thing they aren't doing.

Any ideas?

We've already talked about how you are all saying the same thing. It's already a well-known fact that most dealers are competing on price.

So what aren't they doing that you can start doing today?

Convey value.

Look, everyone on the planet already knows that you're a dealership and that you sell vehicles. They already know that as a retail establishment, you're going to have promotions and special offers.

Sadly, they also already know that they can expect the same experience dealing with you over any other dealership. They are all hesitant, and all still believe (for some reason) that you're just going to tell them what they want to hear to make the sale.

A friend of mine recently shared an article that validates this.

According to the article, nearly nine in 10 people[6] believe that there should be an easier or better way of shopping for their car.

52% say that the excitement of buying a car soon turns to fear of you being taking advantage of them. As a result, only 24% of consumers still feel excited post-purchase while 44% describe themselves as feeling relieved.

Nobody is doing anything differently, though. Everyone is still continuing to advertise the same way, talk about the same things and compete at the same level. And it's scaring the crap out potential buyers.

But what do you think would happen if you stopped trying to compete with surrounding dealerships? What if you started focussing on what makes you unique and providing real value?

Consumers will start to pay attention. Why? Because it's what they are craving and desperately waiting for you to do.

You won't be able to do this the right way until you stop paying such close attention to your competitors.

My point is this:

If you want to separate yourself from the competition and rise above the marketing clutter, you'll need to leave them alone.

Let them continue to quarrel over price. Let them continue to talk about how they have the best team and best vehicles.

Let them continue producing forgettable marketing. Let consumers continue to ignore them.

By pulling yourself off of their playing field, you will be able to move the needle enough in the right direction to get noticed.

More importantly, your competition won't even know what you're doing or how to get started doing it for themselves.

Stop working against yourself. Start leveraging the clutter by changing your focus and direction.

We're going to talk more about how to convey value through marketing later in this book. But for now, you should know that you can use the crappy marketing clutter to your advantage.

Why compete **when you can dominate?**

CHAPTER TWO QUESTIONS

What are some ways that you can leverage the marketing
clutter to your ultimate advantage?

What is one thing that your competition isn't doing
that you can start doing today?

Why is it unhealthy to pay such close attention
to your competition?

THE MARKET IS INCREDIBLY CLUTTERED, AND THAT'S YOUR MOST VALUABLE ASSET

DON'T WAIT, **DOMINATE!**

WILL THIS ACTUALLY WORK FOR ME OR MY DEALERSHIP?

Okay, so you've made it this far, and you might be thinking,

"This sounds logical, but will it actually work for me and my dealership?"

That's a valid question, and the short answer is simple:

YES!

Of course it will.

Throughout the rest of this book, we're going to look at some key marketing concepts that you're probably not doing.

I've already mentioned how these marketing concepts have worked for myself and other marketers. But maybe you're looking for more social proof from inside the dealership?

They are concepts that help dealers like **Tracy Myers**, C.M.D., get more leads in one month than most dealers get in a year.

They are marketing concepts that have helped some of my clients see 30%, 40% or even 50% increases in leads in a 90-day period.

These concepts have helped car sales pros like **Mike Davenport**, **Charles Cannon** or **Robert Wiesman** earn 6-figure incomes.

And that's because there is something very important to

41

understand. Marketing is marketing. There is no new marketing concept out there that somehow only applies to the automotive industry.

It makes me laugh a little when I hear people in the industry talk about automotive digital marketing. They do it in a way that makes it sound like it's not normal marketing. Like it's a new kind of marketing where traditional marketing concepts won't work.

It reminds me of that episode of "The Cosby Show" where Theo makes a long, compelling argument to Heathcliff. His argument is about why he just needs to be accepted as a regular person because maybe that's all he was born to be.

The audience' sympathetic reaction to Theo's speech leads you to believe that Cliff will say what every other TV show dad would've said. "You know son, you're right...I'll accept you for who you are..."

Cue heartfelt music and audience "Awwwwwww"... **NOT!**

Instead, Cliff looks at his son and says,

"Theo...that's the dumbest thing I've ever heard in my life!"

That's the same thought I have when I hear people talk about automotive digital marketing.

Like I just said, **marketing is marketing**. You can do it the right way, or you can do it the wrong way.

But at its core, **marketing is about conveying the right message to the right customer at the right time and in the right tone.**

We're going to cover this more throughout the book and how to do it, so don't worry.

For now, it's important to understand one very important fact.

Automotive customers don't shop for vehicles as regularly as they shop for everything else.

When we talk about automotive consumers, we tend to think that they are exclusively shopping for a vehicle.

That's just **not true.**

What you can learn from pretty much everywhere else on the planet...

Automotive shoppers are every other kind of consumer first. They are web-savvy people who spend crazy amounts of time online each day, week and month.

In 2014 alone, 198 million[7] U.S. consumers purchased something online. That translates to a whopping 78% of Americans aged 15 and older.

Also, Canadians spent over $20 billion[8] dollars shopping online. That's some pretty decent money from my home country that only has 35 million people!

Why am I telling you this?

It demonstrates my point that automotive consumers are every other kind of consumer.

They are using other websites more frequently, and those websites have shifted the way they use the web and what they expect.

Sites like eBay, Amazon, Zappos and pretty much every other e-commerce site all provide similar experiences. They follow similar methodologies. As a result, they condition the expectations of the consumers' online behavior.

When those consumers arrive at a point in their life when they need a vehicle, they go online. What they get when they land on yours or your competitors web site is shocking!

The experience is lacking, the self-centered language is insulting, and most of the time, there isn't enough information to keep people engaged.

Chin up. **Pay Attention!**

I said it earlier, and I'll say it again. Automotive consumers are craving your expertise and wisdom. For most car shoppers, the thought of buying a vehicle can be pretty intimidating.

Consumers feel this way due to a lack of information.

Every day millions of automotive shoppers are going online to research your products and services. The problem is that, in most cases, they can't find the information that will help them make a qualified purchase decision.

Have you ever heard something like this before?:

"Most of the time when a customer comes in to buy, they end up buying something else altogether!" I hear this all the time...

But have you ever considered why that is?

Could it have anything to do with the fact that they can't find information online that qualifies them in the right direction?

Your success in online marketing has everything to do with how much valuable information you produce. People are going online to do research already, but dealers haven't paid attention yet.

Paying attention to the market is one of the first rules of successful business. Find out what the market wants/needs and then fill that need.

Simple.

It's in your best interest to get cracking and figure out exactly what your target audience wants. Here are some ways that you can do that.

1. DISCUSSION FORUMS

Open a web browser and do a Google search for "[your make here] forum". If you're a Chevy dealer, search for "Chevrolet forum".

You'll immediately see different websites online where you can engage with real people. More importantly, you'll be able to see what questions people are asking on a regular basis.

Not only is this incredible to find out what their interests are, this should fill you with ideas to create compelling content. Look to see what forum questions are getting the most action and take note.

2. SOCIAL MEDIA HASHTAGS

You can search for different hashtags on both Twitter and Facebook to see what topics people are talking about.
I use this method every single day to search for and find social conversations that I can join, for a couple of reasons.

First, to get a gauge on what topics people are talking about and see what questions they have.

Second, to offer my expertise if someone is asking a question that I can answer.

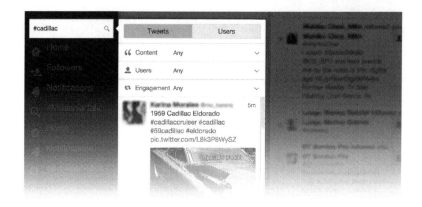

I also pick up new followers on both social networks daily by using them to engage with real people and offer value.

3. EMAIL SURVEY TO PAST CUSTOMERS

Look, just because they are past customers, doesn't mean they aren't also future customers. We all know how important repeat business is.

But past customers are a powerful resource for you. From them, you can find out what interests real drivers of your products have in common.

Using your CRM, take some time to segment your database of customers, dividing them by the vehicle type they have purchased. Then send out an email to each list asking a specific question that's relevant to them.

It could be as simple as this:

SUBJECT:

"I'm dying to know!"

BODY:

"Hi [First name],

I have a quick question for you, and I'm dying to know the answer!

Since the purchase of your [make/model], what feature of the vehicle has become your favorite?

I'd love to hear from you.

Talk soon,
[Your name]"

You see where I'm going with this? Think about how many people you have listed in your CRM database. You're bound to get some feedback from past customers.

How long is it going to take before you catch on?

While recording the 50th episode of The Dealer Playbook Podcast featuring Jay Baeri, I made a statement. I needed to point out an important piece of information that you should understand.

We've been fortunate enough to have some of the greatest marketing minds on the show as guests. Here's a list of just a few:

Tracy Myers
Grant Cardone
Dan Waldschmidt
Greg Rollett
Marcus Sheridan
Jay Baer
Tim Paige
Gary Vaynerchuk

And guess what? They've all been saying the same things about online marketing! How many more marketing gurus need to add their name to the list before you catch on?

There's a reason other marketers in every other industry on

the planet (including automotive) are finding success. They are filling a need. They are giving their audience what they want.

And, as a result, the audience returns the favor and business grows.

You have an unlimited number of audience members. They are going online as we speak. They are searching for topics that will help qualify them to make the right buying decision.

At this exact moment in time, consumers in your market are searching for information that you're currently not providing.

But if you're not doing it, **who is?**

It's time for you to step up. It is time for you stand out.

With that in mind, you're ready to find out what baking a cake can teach you about online marketing…

CHAPTER THREE QUESTIONS

List three ways that you can find out what your customers want.

1.

2.

3.

If you could sit down with me for 30 minutes, what marketing questions about your dealership would you ask?

SUCCESS IS A RECIPE

What would happen if I asked you to bake a cake and only provided you with the ingredients to do so? Do you think you'd be able to do it? Would you be able to guess your way through the process and actually end up with a cake?

First of all, let me just say that if you could, I would be très impressed! Seriously, I'd have to shake your hand!

I'm not saying that I don't think you would eventually figure it out. With enough time and money, I'm sure anyone could figure it out.

But if you're like me, chances are you'd struggle to bake something that even remotely resembled (let alone tasted like) a cake at first.

It's kind of like the situation that many dealers are facing. They have the ingredients they need to make success happen, but much of it gets left to guesswork. The outcome rarely resembles the expectations and is often more expensive than it needs to be.

Since we know that you already have the ingredients needed to thrive online, there's only one way to avoid the guesswork.

Have a recipe **to follow.**

We're not talking about any old recipe, though. You need a recipe that will deliver the intended result.

Not all recipes are created equal

There isn't one all-encompassing recipe that will magically work for your online marketing. Trust me, there are many that think there is, but my experience has proven otherwise.

Believe me, I'm not trying to make this sound more difficult. I just want you to understand that there are different recipes depending on what you want to "bake".

It kind of sounds like a "duh" no-brainer when I say this, but the only way for you to follow the right recipe is to know what you want to accomplish first!

And no, it's not as easy as saying, "I want more traffic, leads and sales!", either. Of course you want more traffic leads and sales – what dealer doesn't.

But if more traffic, leads and sales is your goal what methods and strategies will you use to achieve success?

Do you want more website traffic? If so, from where? Organic search? Social media? Paid advertising? Traditional advertising?

It's not enough to just say that the goal is more traffic. You need to identify the source of that traffic. That traffic source has a recipe for you to follow.

For example, driving traffic from organic SEO is different than driving traffic from social media. Of course, the objective is to drive traffic, but you'd need to follow different recipes to make it happen.

Any decent baker will tell you that a recipe book is worthless if you don't know what you want to bake.

And this is the predicament that so many dealers find themselves. When the goal is as vague as, *"I want traffic, leads and sales"* it's about as good as saying, *"I want cake".*

Well, what kind of cake do you want? That's the only way you will be able to measure success, and meet expectations.

If you had a craving for chocolate cake but followed the recipe for a lemon cake, would you be happy? I mean, both are cake after all...

How does this apply to the dealer world?

If your goal is to get more leads, but you're not quite sure what type of leads you want, how will you know what recipe to follow.

Don't tell me that you just want any old leads, either. If you want to grow your business, build a happy customer base, it's time for you to identify the type of leads you want to attract.

Are they new car leads or used car leads? Are they finance leads or leasing leads? Are they bad credit leads? Are they service or parts leads? Are they trade-in leads?

What type of leads are they? You can't just throw each of them in the same bucket and hope there is a blanket recipe for attracting each. Leads aren't leads. They are people with varying interests and concerns.

As you can imagine, someone looking at used vehicles is vastly different than someone looking for services.

And where are you going to get these leads?

The Curve Ball

You can't mix recipes and hope for something that tastes good (unless you're willing to experiment).

But why experiment when there are proven recipes for success?

I hear this all the time from dealers. *"I want more leads..."* yet when the leads come in, (and I love this part), I often hear,

Wait, what?!? What does that have to do with anything? You asked for more leads, and **more leads arrived**, but you're not happy because website traffic hasn't increased?

I thought we were following the recipe for more leads! So what does it matter if website traffic has increased or not? That's not the result we were working to achieve.

Do you see where I'm going with this?

There is a recipe for success online based on what you want to accomplish.

Yes, you can follow more than one recipe and run them alongside one another, so long as you know what result the recipes will bring you.

Don't think that the *"more leads"* recipe will increase your traffic from organic search results. Especially if the recipe didn't call for more traffic from organic search.

But while we're on the topic, let me just say this. I've helped dealers see a decrease in website traffic while getting **MORE** leads than they've ever received...

So again, stop thinking that there is one single recipe for online success. There are recipes (plural) for you to follow based on what you want. You just need to know what it is that you want to begin with...

One last thing about the Ingredients...

At this point, you should understand that being successful online is all about following a recipe. You have all the ingredients you need, but there is one last thing to consider.

There is a trick to following a recipe that will empower you to get consistent results.

Each of the ingredients must get added in the right sequence. In fact, the entire recipe depends on it.

But following the recipe also comes with it the temptation to look for shortcuts. For example, some may find the length of the recipe discouraging because they need to find some measure of success immediately, or for less money...

Have you ever felt this way? I know I have.

I've learned a valuable lesson about shortcuts from personal experience, though.

Shortcuts always lead to **'Long Cuts'.**

In other words, if you try and find a shortcut to success online, you will end up paying for your mistakes in some way, shape or form.

Don't take this the wrong way. I'm not trying to brainwash you into believing that you should always choose the most expensive ingredients (providers, agencies, websites etc.) either.

I do believe, however, that getting the job done right the first time is the best and least expensive way.

Ok...The last LAST thing about the ingredients...

Later in this book we're going to explore the ingredients in more detail, but for now here's the last LAST thing I'd like to share with you.

When it comes to online marketing, you're going to need the same core ingredients. They won't change!

In fact, you'll find yourself recycling them even for different recipes. The sequence that you use them will vary from recipe to recipe, but in and of themselves, they will not change.

Good news right?

I've spoken to so many dealers who get worried that doing online marketing means they will have to keep forking out more cash for new "stuff".

That's simply not the case.

With that in mind, I think we're ready to explore each of the ingredients in more detail.

Remember, the problem up to this point hasn't been that you've had all the wrong ingredients. It's that you haven't been using the ingredients you have in the right way.

All that is about to change. **Buckle up...**

CHAPTER FOUR QUESTIONS

What will help you avoid the guesswork when it comes to online marketing?

What are some ways that shortcuts turn into 'longcuts'?

How should you apply the "ingredients" of online marketing?

INGREDIENTS OF ONLINE SUCCESS

(plus how to use them)

DON'T WAIT, **DOMINATE!**

HOW TO ATTRACT THE **RIGHT CUSTOMER** AND REPEL THE WRONG ONE

Wait a minute. Do you mean to tell me that there is such a thing as a **'wrong customer'**?

Why yes. **Yes, there is.**

In fact, that's the whole idea behind great marketing in the first place: To attract the **RIGHT** customers and **REPEL** the wrong ones.

Let me explain…

About a year ago, I was watching television with my wife when a "Skechers Tone-ups" sneakers commercial came on.

In the commercial, there's a young blonde chick dancing around the house in her underwear.

With several quick shots of the blonde's booty, I was curious what the commercial could be promoting. And no, it wasn't because there was a blonde chick dancing around the house in her underwear.

The caption - **"Love Your Butt!"**

The concept is that these sneakers will help tone and shape your butt.

As I sat there thinking about how ridiculous the product was, I could almost see my wife inching closer to the television. She was intrigued and attracted by the message like a mosquito to one of those blue shiny zapper lights.

I mean, what could be better than butt-shaping and toning running shoes, right?

WRONG! Well, at least wrong for me.

My wife felt compelled at the same time that I was being repelled.

That's not to say that the messaging in the commercial had enough force to drive me completely out of the shoe market, though. It was just enough to repel my interest level in butt-toning sneakers.

But from this example alone, you can see that Skechers achieved their objective. They attracted the right (or intended) audience and repelled the WRONG (or non-intended) audience.

Here's another example:

I was scrolling through my Facebook feed one day when I came across a rather interesting post.

A friend of mine was ranting about how many customers online shopping site, Zuliliy.com must be losing because they make people sign up for membership before they can shop.

When I clicked to view the comments on this post, I found that several people in automotive marketing agreed with him.

I was shocked that they weren't seeing the bigger picture of what Zulily is doing with that signup mechanism.

I commented on his post by stating that depending on Zulily's objectives, this may be a genius move on their part. His reply made me chuckle a little. His argument to me was that **HE** is Zulily's target demographic, and if they want people to shop there, Zulily had better change things up.

Here's where it gets interesting...

When I looked at Zulily's 'about page' on their website, this is the first paragraph of the page:

*"...something special every day Zulily is a retailer obsessed with bringing **MOMS** special finds every day – all at incredible prices..."*

I had to post this to the comments.

I'm no rocket scientist, but I'm pretty sure **HE** is not a **MOM**. That means that he is also not their target demographic, as he thought.

Zulily has an interest in the "mom" demographic and aims to provide the best deals on great products using the membership model.

Point served.

You see, Zulily is executing a strategic marketing initiative that attracts the RIGHT customer and REPELS the wrong customer.

So, here's the golden question:

How does this apply to your dealership?

How can you create a strategic marketing initiative that will help you attract the right customers to your store?

For starters, you need to understand that like the Skechers' commercials, every car you have was designed for a specific audience.

Not everyone wants or needs to drive cars, trucks, Vans or SUVs. Not every customer is a bad credit customer or a lease customer. Each vehicle or service you provide was designed with a specific target audience in mind.

We call these: **Consumer Segments**.

In other words, groups of consumers who share common interests or needs.

If you create website content that focuses on a particular make or model, don't assume that it will attract everyone. Understand that the marketing you do will, by nature, repel certain customers.

That's not to say that they will get turned off from buying vehicles altogether. It just means that they will get turned off from the wrong vehicle or service for them.

Focus on creating relevant content that will help you attract the intended audience.

Is Anything Sticking?

You know that old saying, *"throw it against the wall and see what sticks"*?

I hate it.

But I also love it...

I hate it because it's the reason that the market is so cluttered. Everyone is saying anything and everything, and it has created marketing chaos.

I love it because it's the reason the market is so cluttered today than it ever was back in the day. Everyone is saying anything and everything, and it has created a massive opportunity for you to dominate.

You just have to say the right thing to the right consumer.

Great marketing is about being something of value to somebody, not worthless to everybody.

Don't feel like you have to engage in saying the same thing as every other dealership. Don't feel like you have to market yourself the same way that they are.

After all, don't you think that if it were a right way of doing things, the data would confirm it?

I mean, let's get real. Everyone is doing the same crappy marketing online, but everyone is still complaining about how bad things are.

I'm no mathematician, but I'd say things aren't adding up.

Each message that you share, whether through your website, video or social media will resonate in a different way for specific consumer segments.

Some will like it, others won't. As long as you understand that there isn't a blanket ad or piece of content that will attract absolutely everyone equally, you're off to a great start.

We're going to take a much deeper look at consumer segments in the next chapter, but for now we need to cover one more thing.

What Makes Great Marketing?

We've already talked about how great marketing both attracts and repels customers.

So what else is there?

There are several elements that are important for you to understand to get the most out of your marketing efforts. Each element will strengthen and enhance your ability to dominate and **THRIVE** online.

I guess the best place to start is first to talk about what great marketing **is not.**

At some point in the history of our industry, nay planet, some lazy idiot needed a smack upside the head! (I'd like to believe that if the smack was hard enough that we wouldn't be left with this ridiculous pandemic of pathetic marketing that now plagues us.)

It's the crappy marketing that we've been talking about up to this point, that most dealers are still doing. It's the kind of marketing that started in the newspapers, but has made its way over to the internet.

It makes me sad...in a geeky kind of way.

Let's look at a couple of examples.

SMOKIN DEAL ON A 12 LIFTED DURAMAX ONLY 75KM!!! $45,900 GET AT US ASAPPPP!!!!!

WHY ARE YOU YELLING AT ME? DO YOU THINK THAT THIS WILL SOMEHOW GET MORE QUALIFIED BUYERS TO PAY ATTENTION?

2006 Chevrolet Trailblazer Ext LS 130,960 miles $5,995

Why resort to the pricing game right out of the gates? Does this give you more leverage, especially when your competitors are all doing the same thing?

Take a drive down the auto-mile and all you'll see are signs, banners, balloons and the big gorilla promoting what? **PRICE!**

And like I said - it's transferred online.

Take a look at the PPC ads out there (maybe even your own). Most of them are price driven. And even when they don't specifically focus on price, they do always tend to focus on getting a better deal. At the end of the day, the message is still about price!

Look at most dealer social media posts. Pictures of inventory and what? **PRICE!**

Of course! Price is the only thing you have to leverage when you're not conveying any value.

But what if I told you that a tiny fraction (like 5% or so) of the market were price shoppers? What about the other 95%[9] of the market who are still in other phases of the buying process?

67

By now, you should recognize this as cluttered crappy marketing.

Please, dear Lord, **make it stop!**

If you want to attract the right high-quality customers, things have to change. When you focus on creating and demonstrating value, things will shift in your favor.

Who do you know that is currently conveying value these days? 3rd party sites?

Really? You're allowing 3rd party sites to dictate the education of your potential customers?!? **This has to stop immediately.**

Okay, my rant is over. Let's move on to what great marketing IS...

Great Marketing is Emotional and Memorable

When you look at the most memorable marketing out there, it's often emotional. Emotional marketing is the kind that rarely gets ignored and helps build rapport and trust quickly.

Mothers Against Drunk Driving has some of the best emotional marketing I've seen.

I can still remember the M.A.D.D ad on the back of my 8th-grade agenda. It was an image of a crumpled up sports car with the caption, "This car still turns heads!" That was more than 20 years ago, and I still remember it!

If you'd like to see how impactful and emotional their advertising is, do a Google image search for *"mothers against drunk driving ads"*, and scroll through the images.

Take a look at what you're doing right now with your marketing. Is anything about it memorable? If not, take this as an opportunity to hit the drawing board.

Great Marketing is Laser Targeted

We've already talked about how you need to be something valuable to somebody, not worthless to everybody.

We're going to take a deeper look at this concept in the next chapter. For now, I want you to think about the Skechers commercial and the Zulily.com website examples from earlier.

It's much easier to speak with people about the things they care about or have an interest in. It's common sense! I mean, do me a favor and think back to the last boring conversation you had with somebody. You likely don't remember the topic, but I'm sure you remember the person and the occasion.

You probably remember how boring they were and how you tried every way possible to get out of the conversation carrying on…

That's the same thing that's happening with your consumers. They may not remember what you were trying to talk about, but they do remember you and that you had nothing interesting to say. Make sense?

Great Marketing is about Giving

Don't read too deep into this.

Often when I tell dealers that they should focus on giving more than they take, they get a little worried. At first they don't see how that will benefit them.

Many still fail to realize how this can benefit them. If you feel this way, don't worry. I used to feel the same way!

Something powerful happens when you give away your best information for free.

Your credibility, authority, and expertise go through the roof in an instant!

Do you want your market to know you as the undisputed expert? Give away so much free, valuable, great information that they won't be able to deny you!

Giving consumers your best may sound counter-intuitive to many dealers and business owners out there. Especially because most people feel that they've earned the right to charge money for their expertise.

But how will your customers know you're the expert if you don't reveal what you know? Your customers won't know that you have their best interests in mind until you prove otherwise.

Some of the greatest marketing minds in the world, such as Seth Godin, Gary Vaynerchuk, Grant Cardone and Ryan Deiss (to name a few) are great examples of over-delivering value. That way when it's time to ask for the sale, consumers respect what they bring to the table.

Can you see how massive **the opportunity** is here?

If not, let's take a quick look at the flip side of this.

If you don't subscribe to the idea of giving value, or focus on being valuable to somebody, what does that say about you?

I tried every which way to think about how to not say that you're being selfish, but there is no better word for you.

When you don't give, it conveys the message that all you care about is yourself. But isn't that the exact message we're trying to avoid?

The auto industry keeps getting slammed with negative press about its self-centered nature. Remember the article that I mentioned earlier which stated that nine in 10 shoppers think there should be a better way to buy a car.

Of those surveyed, **66% agree that car salespeople are self-centered and out for themselves.** Only 22% described their car dealers as trustworthy.

And to make the point again, don't forget this:

Most consumers feel ill-equipped or too intimidated to negotiate with a car dealer. **52%** say that the excitement of buying a car soon turns to fear of being taken advantage of while **44%** say they feel relieved that the whole process is over!

Think about that for a minute. Customers experience fear and stress as a result of the way dealers currently do business!

On top of that, most dealers are delivering a mixed message. There is a big disconnect between what the website says and what it delivers.

For example, does your website say anything about providing better service than your competitors? Does it talk about your top-trained team of professionals?

How can you make those claims when you're not providing any value? Surely a top-trained professional would go out of their way to over-deliver value, wouldn't they?

By not giving, you are confusing the heck out of your customers. You're saying one thing and delivering nothing.

Think about the elements of great marketing that we've just discussed. Are you doing any of them? If not, don't wait.

You can audit your current marketing efforts with one question:

"Would I find this valuable?"

As I said, it's common sense. You need to put yourself in the customers shoes and identify with them.

Give them what they want.

As you do this, the gap between you and the competition will grow fast. They won't have a clue what you're doing or how you're doing it!

You will have
a greater
ability to
**attract the
right customers**
and **repel the
wrong ones.**

CHAPTER FIVE QUESTIONS

What makes great marketing?

Why is it beneficial to repel the wrong customer?

DON'T WAIT, **DOMINATE!**

MARKET SEGMENTATION
WINS THE DAY

In the last chapter, we spent a lot of time talking about how to attract the right customer and repel the wrong one. But what if I told you that the wrong customer could also be the right customer?

Yes. You read that correctly.

Depending on the message that you share, everyone has the potential of being the right customer. In fact, the only thing separating them from becoming the right customer is the message that you share with them.

Just like my example in the previous chapter. I was the wrong customer for Skechers' tone-ups, but that doesn't mean I would never need a new pair of shoes. It just means that I would never have a need for those shoes in particular.

The easiest and best way to make sure that every wrong customer has the potential of becoming the right customer is to segment the market.

Market segmentation is a common practice where a broad set of consumers gets divided into smaller groups. Each smaller group gets made up of consumers who share common interests or needs.

Most dealers group people into the broad category of *'people who buy vehicles'*. While there's nothing inaccurate about that, it helps if you dig a little deeper. Especially if you want to impact the market.

To segment the market properly, you need to take the broad

group of consumers and divide them into smaller groups who share common needs.

For example, Seniors will have different needs or interests from young families. Young families have different interests or needs than college students. Make sense?

But here's why market segmentation is powerful.

When you group people by interests and needs, it is much easier for you to know what to talk about. The things that interest them!

What a **novel idea!**

You mean to tell me that when I talk to people about the things they care about, they pay attention? Of course!

Now that you know this, doesn't it seem kind of, well... simple?

But this is one of the biggest problems that dealers face. They try and speak to everyone, and as a result, they speak to no-one.

Remember that great marketing is about being laser focused and over-delivering value. How can you achieve this if you have no clue who you're speaking to and about what topic?

Also don't forget that a best practice in business is to identify a problem and then provide the solution. If you haven't segmented the market, how will you know what the problems are?

OEMs segment the market like a Boss

Every single vehicle that the OEMs engineer get built with a specific market segment in mind. They know who the vehicle is for before it even touches the assembly line.

They invest millions of dollars into market research to help them understand the needs of various market segments.

Doing so helps them align the marketing of that vehicle with an audience that will resonate most with it. They have a buying profile for every vehicle in their lineup.

Think about the last Ford F-150 commercial you saw. Did it depict a peaceful drive into the backcountry with a young family who enjoyed a picnic followed by a frolic through the meadow? **Not!**

Denis Leary's gritty narration overlays images of a dirty truck at a work site, hauling a load – men with hard hats and shovels. Dirt. Grit. Hard work!

The voice of the commercial penetrates the audience by describing the F-150 in the world that they can understand. It shows how the truck will solve their problems and make their job easier.

Can you imagine what the F-150 commercials would be like if Ford didn't segment the market?

The takeaway here is twofold.

First, that the vehicles you sell are built with the needs and interests of specific market segments.

Second, that all the marketing messages from the OEMs are designed to resonate with the right audience.

Segmenting is the missing link

I was having a conversation with a colleague a few years ago about how to market effectively. He made a comment that didn't sound right to me then, and still doesn't.

We were talking about how much competition there is out there and how the marketing is all the same. He said, *"It doesn't matter who has the best product, or who does things first. It matters who does things loudest."*

In other words, be as loud as you possibly can in the market to get people's attention. The more attention you can get, the better off you'll be.

I get where he's coming from. I mean, it sounds logical, doesn't it?

But what happens when you're loud if you're broadcasting the wrong message? What if you don't know who your audience is and you say things that don't resonate with them?

You'd be making a fool out of yourself, and you'd be doing it louder than anyone else out there! That's what would happen.

You can be as loud as you want, but if your message doesn't resonate with anyone, your decibels are falling on deaf ears.

Segmenting is the missing link from your current marketing efforts. It's one of the reasons that the market is so cluttered. It's one of the reasons that dealers all say the same thing. They don't know who they are speaking to!

But don't worry, because this is where everything starts to turn around for you. When you segment the market, you will be able to craft messaging that turns the wrong customer into the right one.

Get to Know Your Audience(s)

The success of everything you do online depends on how well you know your audiences. What makes them tick? What are they interested in? What moves them to action?

Knowing your audience is one of the most important aspects of marketing. In fact, it's where everything begins. I mean, why would you ever develop a product or service without first knowing who it's for?

When you know your target audience, your ability to build rapport and trust with them goes through the roof! You can provide more value because you'll be talking about things that they want to hear or learn about.

Getting to know your target audience this day in age is much easier than ever! Let me explain...

Do you know what makes the best conversationalist? I learned this when I read Dale Carnegie's "How to Win Friends and Influence People". He says,

"**We have two ears and one mouth** – use them accordingly.[10]"

The main takeaway: Be a good listener, encourage others to talk about themselves. We should listen twice as much as we speak!

Okay, but how does this have anything to do with getting to know your audience online?

This might sound geeky, but whatever! Go with me on this for a minute, okay? You see, the internet is the greatest listener EVER.

That's all it does, day in and day out. Listen.

But not just any listening. Listening to the tune of 3+ Billion[11] Google searches per day.

Think about it. We talk to the internet, and it listens. It then delivers what we want. It repeats this process until we finish talking at it.

It's not just listening though. It's listening and then remembering.

Everything we say gets stored in memory. As a marketer, you can use the internet's memory to help you understand what billions of people have an interest in.

Pretty cool right? You can use technology to help you learn so much about your customers before they even meet you in person!

Google Trends is a powerful tool that I use to help me understand what people are searching for online. It's a free resource that Google provides where you can see the topics that get searched for most often.

You can even break out the information by region to get a closer look at what's hot in your area. When you find a topic that has a lot of searches, you can use that information to create content that consumers will want to see.

Market Segment Exercise

At this point, you should understand how important segmenting the market is to your online success.

But you're likely wondering how to get started segmenting the market.

So let's take a look at a quick exercise that you can do over your morning cup of coffee.

Following these steps will give you greater clarity about who your marketing is targeting. That way you'll be able to craft messages that will break through the clutter and resonate with potential buyers.

Are you ready? Here we go!

STEP 1:

In the middle of a blank sheet of paper write, **"People who purchase vehicles"** in the center and then draw a circle around it. Here's mine:

Next, write as many groups of people surrounding the circle as you can. These might include (but not limited to):

Seniors
Young Families
Construction workers
College students and Millennials
Military
Civil Servants (Police, Fire, Paramedic)
Women Buyers
Minorities

STEP 2:

Select one group of people at a time and write down as many needs, wants or interests as you can.

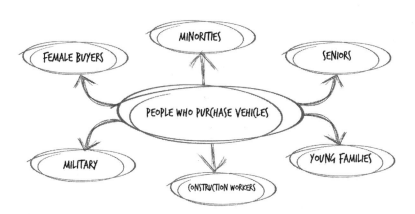

81

This is also where you can use Google Trends or similar tools to find out what people are already searching for.

For example, Seniors might have interest in the following:

Ease of entry and exit
Towing capacity
Reliability
Safety
Luxury

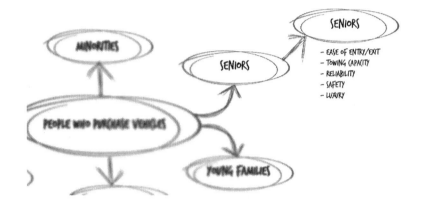

STEP 3:

The final step is to align each group's wants/needs/interests with a vehicle that best fits the criteria.

Using the Seniors segment as an example, what vehicle(s) do you currently have in stock that fill the needs listed in step 2?

List them out...

Then repeat this process for each of the segments that you have listed.

Like I said. This quick and easy exercise will help you understand your potential customers with clarity.

The idea is that this will help you know who to speak to and what topics to speak to them about.

The last thing to do once you've completed this exercise is to list out a variety of topic ideas based on your findings.

Using this information you are positioning yourself to rise above the clutter and dominate the market.

There is no compensation for failing to segment the market. Your effectiveness as a marketer depends on it.

CHAPTER SIX QUESTIONS

What is market segmentation?

Why is getting to know your audience crucial
to online marketing?

What market segments does your brand(s) cover?

DON'T WAIT, **DOMINATE!**

OVER DELIVER VALUE...
ALWAYS!

I've said this before, and I'll say it again. Every single day, millions of automotive shoppers are going online to research vehicles.

They are visiting your website in search for answers to their questions and solutions to their problems.

To validate this, do me a favor and take a peek at your Google Analytics (which we're going to look at in more detail later). How many visitors were on your site in the last 30 days?

Chances are that you've had more visitors to your website in the last 30 days than you did to your showroom.

Think about that for a minute. I've spoken with many business who get depressed when they see a low number of visitors.

But that number (no matter how high or low it is) is irrelevant because it's likely still more than you get to your physical store each month.

If you're worried about a low number of site visitors, shift your focus a little. Rather than thinking in terms of the quantity of site visits, think in terms of the quality of site visits.

After all, millions of visits each month won't make a difference to your bottom line if none of them convert into leads. Do you agree?

You don't need millions of visits to make big things happen. You don't even need tons of new traffic to thrive online.

There is this misconception that by getting more [new] traffic, that things will be better. I worry when I hear how much some dealers spend to get more traffic.

What you need is to leverage the traffic that is already coming to your site. You need to squeeze every last ounce of action out of those that are coming to check out what you have to offer, first.

The point I'm trying to make is that you're getting traffic to your virtual store on a daily basis. People in your market are already interested in what you have going on. But while they're on your site, you're busy focusing on how to get more people to your site.

It's backward thinking. It reminds me of a friends birthday party that I went to as a kid. I was the coolest guest at his party until the newer guests arrived. Then I was just, well...old news.

Are you treating your existing site visitors like they are old news? If you are, things need to change.

There is one surefire way to leverage existing website visitors to get more high-quality leads. It's something that I've already mentioned several times throughout the book.

Provide **value.**

So far, each of the examples I've shared has lacked the one thing that turns visitors into leads. The lack of value out there is the reason there's so much crappy marketing.

Value is what gets the attention of high-quality buyers. It empowers them to make purchase decisions much faster because it makes them feel more confident.

Remember the article that I referenced earlier? What was the biggest problem that consumers face when purchasing a vehicle?

They are fearful because they feel ill-equipped to negotiate with the dealer. If they were armed with information, do you think they would feel that same fear?

I hope you don't find that as a trick question. I hope you're not thinking that feeling ill-equipped to negotiate is the perfect way to sell.

If so, please put this book down, look yourself in the mirror and repeat these words:

I'M A JERK!

Change the way you think. If you can empower your customers by providing value, all you need to do is validate what they've learned when they visit you in person.

That validation will sell you more vehicles, products, and services faster than anything you're doing now. It gives you the framework to be agreeable with the customer on facts, rather than agreeing with them to sell them something.

I get it, though. What exactly will the customer find valuable?

Even if you know who they are and what topics they're interested in, what can you deliver that will satisfy them? What can you produce that will shape their purchase decisions and make them feel more confident?

This is where most dealers get stuck with their online marketing because they don't know what to do or how to get started conveying the kind of value that gets noticed.

This is also the reason so many dealers pay such close attention to their competitors. When they see the competition doing something (anything) that they aren't, it's perceived as them doing the right thing.

But like we've already discussed, if your competitors were doing the right kind of marketing, why is everyone complaining about how slow business is? It doesn't add up, does it?

Creating and conveying value is one of the most difficult aspects of online marketing to master. It requires a lot of energy and work. You have to be involved in the process even if you've contracted someone else to do the work for you.

Here's the good news: It doesn't require any more or any less energy and work than you're already putting in. It just requires that you refocus that energy into something that will work long-term.

It's not easy, but it is more than worth it. That's the genius of creating and conveying value, though. If it were easy to do, everyone would be doing it.

That's the whole reason you should commit and get moving. Don't wait for someone else to become your market's expert. Start dominating today by creating so much value that people won't be able to deny your expertise.

There's an even bigger **upside to all of this.**

We talk so much in the industry about the length of time it takes consumers to make a buying decision. Currently, we're sitting at an average of 3 months[12].

But what if you could shorten that duration by simply extending so much value that the consumer felt comfortable deciding sooner? And better yet, choosing you!

We know that auto shoppers are doing more online research today than ever before. Google's, "Digital Drives Auto

Shopping", reveals that consumers use 24 Research touch points on average.

So why not meet them where they already are with the information that they expect?

You see, the internet has added a layer of transparency to the buying process that consumers now demand. They are much more sophisticated than we're giving them credit for.

Remember in Chapter 3 when we talked about how automotive consumers aren't exclusive?

I mentioned that automotive shoppers are every other kind of consumer, first...

This is important to keep in mind, especially now. The other websites that people visit on a regular basis shape their online expectations.

That means that by the time they land on your website, their expectations are sky high.

The problem is that when they visit your website, they aren't finding the information that they want. As a result, they are moving from your site to other sites that have the information.

And like I mentioned earlier, why would you ever want 3rd party sites (or your competitors) to dictate your customer's education?

Since we've already established that people are more receptive when you speak to them about topics they're interested in, your mission is simple.

Talk to them about the topics that they are interested in.

Look, the fastest way for you to build trust with potential buyers is to give them exactly what they want.

Don't hold back on information thinking that it will somehow compel them to do business with you. That's an old school strategy that doesn't work this day in age.

Focus on providing so much information that people start raising their hand and saying, *"I'm here, give me more!"*

Not just any information, though. Give them the best that you have to offer. The reason is simple...

People do business with people they both **like and trust.**

When you focus on providing loads of value, consumers will naturally begin to respect what you have to say. You'll be able to shape their purchase decisions because of your expertise.

When I share this with the dealers that I consult, at first they are hesitant to accept this 'new' way of doing business. Look, I get it. It sounds foreign compared to anything they (or you) have ever done before.

But this is what your customers crave. It's the whole reason they are going online in the first place. They want valuable information.

So stop getting in your way, and stop getting in theirs! **Always over deliver value.**

Stop using the word 'value' unless you're going to tell us what it is!

Trust me, I was even getting to the point where I was sick of using the word! But I had to make sure the point was delivered. Value is the differentiator, especially when it's geared towards the right audience!

At the end of the day, the value will get delivered via the content you create.

Think about it, what would the internet be without content?

What would Google be without content? After all, content is the whole reason Google even exists.

I mean, can you imagine doing a Google search and getting nothing but a blank white page returned to you?

Content pretty much fuels everything online.

Those 3+ billion Google searches that happen each day are seeking out, yup you guessed it, content!

A percentage of those 3+ billion Google searches are your potential customers. They are the ones that go online to research vehicles, browse your web site and, hopefully, submit leads.

But they're not submitting leads as much as you'd like because why? They aren't finding any valuable content!

The content comes in a variety of forms. Each of which can be leveraged and included on or around your dealer (or personal) website. Here are just a few:

Content/Landing pages
Email Marketing
Blogging
Video
Audio
Images and Infographics
Social Media Posts and Social Proof (Testimonials)
Reviews

The beauty is that you can create several types of content and make them work with one another.

For example, here is a simple content strategy that I use to generate new traffic and leads.
Remember the exercise from Chapter 6? The following section is where we're going to put it to use.

You need to keep in mind the market segment that you'll be

creating content for. In this example, we're using the Young Family segment.

Young families often need a vehicle with more space, fuel economy, seating, and entertainment. Using that information, what vehicles in your inventory meet those requirements?

Minivans and SUVs.

With that in mind, let me show you a conversion path that will generate higher quality vehicle buyers for you.

Ready?

First, you need a clearly defined outcome. What action do you want young families to take when they consume your content?

Since this whole book is about how to stand out from the clutter and dominate online, I'm going to assume that you want them to convert into a lead.

But it's not as simple as just saying, **"I want more leads."** You need to define the path you want the customer to take before they can become a high-quality lead.

A common mistake that most dealers make (and some vendors) is that they don't create a path (or funnel). They create a page on their site and drop a meaningless contact form on it as if that's all it will take.

But we're talking about over delivering value, so the **'plop and smear'**[13] strategy won't work.

Think about the information you want them to know. We always talk about how consumers know more these days because of the internet, so why not jump into the mix? Why not take total control and be the provider of information?

Why continue to be acted upon? There's no sense in it.

If consumers are going to do their research anyway, why not

be the one who leads them down a pathway of learning?

After all, the more you over deliver on valuable information, the higher your credibility and authority will rise.

So here's an example path that you can implement when creating content for your website:

To get the most out of this conversion path (funnel), you will need to make a couple of minor tweaks to your website. Don't worry, they won't affect your OEM compliance.

Since we're still talking about young families, put yourself in their shoes. Ask yourself what you would find more compelling when visiting a dealer site.

Objective:
Get consumer segment to click the link to visit the content page

Currently, all dealer websites look and feel the same. The calls-to-action are the same. When a customer enters your site, what do they see?

New vehicles, used vehicles, get pre-approved and service. **SNOOZE!**

What if you had calls to action that speak directly to your target segment?
If you had to choose between, **"Used Vehicles on Special"** or **"Top 5 Reasons Young Families Prefer the Toyota Sienna"** which would you click on? Don't forget, think like the young family!

That's the first step. Make sure that there is a CTA clearly visible to your market segment that will attract their attention.

Once they click, you need to deliver them exactly what they expect. Information on the "Top 5 Reasons Young Families Prefer the Toyota Sienna". I call this a **"VCP"** or Value Content Page.

That value content page should include a relevant call-to-action that links to a comparison page. Something like,

"See how the Sienna stacks up".

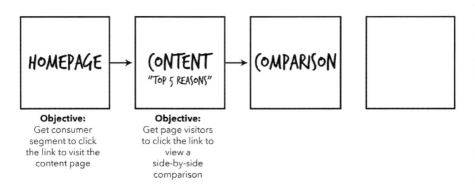

Objective:
Get consumer segment to click the link to visit the content page

Objective:
Get page visitors to click the link to view a side-by-side comparison

When the customer arrives on the comparison page, make sure that it provides them non-biased, non sales-related information. Build trust by delivering exactly what you say you will. No more, no less.

You then need to include a relevant CTA on this page for them to view the current in-stock Sienna inventory.

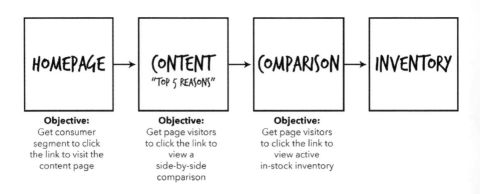

Objective:
Get consumer segment to click the link to visit the content page

Objective:
Get page visitors to click the link to view a side-by-side comparison

Objective:
Get page visitors to click the link to view active in-stock inventory

From the inventory pages, the customer will have the opportunity to submit a lead or call your store.

That's a simple path from start to finish. Can you see how this differs from what you might currently be doing?

Instead of rushing the customer to a sales pitch, you are carefully maneuvering them from one phase of the buying process to another. You are over-delivering value before you ask for their information.

The psychology behind this is that every time you move them from one place to another, you give them exactly what you said you would.

What better way can you think of to build trust between you and your virtual visitor than doing what you say you're going to do?

Are your competitors doing any of this? Heck no! Again, if they were, they wouldn't be complaining so much about not getting high-quality leads.

Want to know how to supercharge the process?

Using the same topic, "Top 5 Reasons...", follow this process:

First, create a vehicle video outlining each of the five reasons. Make sure the video is well thought out. Speak to the camera as if it's your customer standing there with you. Make it personable, and don't be afraid to let your personality shine. **Next,** have the audio from the video transcribed. After a few minutes of cleaning it up into written language, you now have a new blog post for your blog.

Upload the video to your YouTube channel, and make sure you include the link to the blog post. Also be sure to embed the video in the blog post itself.

*** PAUSE *** at this point, you now have a video, audio, and blog. That's three pieces of valuable content.

*** UNPAUSE ***

Next, post the video on Facebook, Twitter, and other social networks. Be sure to include a link back to the blog post on your website.

Once you've done all that, you have a piece of content that you can include in your email messaging to relevant potential buyers. Grab a snippet from the blog post and quote it in your email with a link back to it.

*** PAUSE *** We're now at five pieces of content...and it all came from a single topic idea. Pretty crazy, right?

Trust me when I tell you, I'm not holding anything back. That's a simple content strategy and conversion path (funnel) that I use to help deliver much higher quality leads.

Those that make it to the end of the path have followed you where you wanted them to go. That means that they are supremely interested in what you have to offer or else they wouldn't have stuck around.

Why You Won't Do Any of This

Content creation can be overwhelming without the right process in place. If you want to dominate your market, you need to commit to creating content on a regular basis.

This is where most people fall short.

But just because you need to be consistent, doesn't mean it needs to be overwhelming. Most of the time when people get overwhelmed, it's because they lack structure.

So the way to make sure that you can create content on a regular basis is to schedule time for it.

Set aside an hour each week, on the same day and schedule it as your content creation time.

When you start posting valuable content on a regular basis, your competition won't be able to keep up. They won't even know where to start.

The more consistent you are, the larger the gap between you and them will grow.

One last thought...

In episode 15 of **The Dealer Playbook Podcast**, Robert Wiesman and I were interviewing International Business Expert, Grant Cardone.

During the episode, Grant said something profound.

*"Content isn't king. **Eyes are king!**"*

It took me a minute to process because at first, it seemed to contradict what I believed was true.

It might even sound like it contradicts what we've spent time talking about in this chapter...

But as I sat there thinking about it, I realized that he was right!

CHAPTER SEVEN QUESTIONS

What's the best way to convey value through your website?

How many lead conversion paths are on your current website?

What pages on your site could you use to deliver more value?
List them below.

OVER DELIVER VALUE... ALWAYS

YOU DON'T HAVE A
TRAFFIC PROBLEM

Nobody online ever has a traffic problem. They just don't.

You don't have traffic problems either.

You might have measurement problems (which we'll dive into in chapter 9). You might have a *'not willing to pay for traffic'* problem, visibility problems or even sales problems.

Those problems are much different than
having a traffic problem.

And that's because **traffic problems** don't exist.

Think about it. 40%[14] of the world's population has access to the internet. That's over 3 Billion people! If you're in North America, it's almost a guarantee that everyone in your market has access to the world wide web.

Google, Facebook, Twitter and LinkedIn (to name a few) are all willing to send you traffic. On top of that, Every person that has access to the internet has the potential to be your traffic.

Getting more traffic to your website doesn't make sense until you know how to leverage existing traffic.

That's not to say that you should never focus on getting more traffic to your site. I'm just saying that your existing site traffic is the perfect test bed to make sure that the value you create is well received.

You wouldn't want to risk driving traffic to a site that underperforms, or conveys the wrong message, would you?

There is no point in building upward if you don't have a solid foundation to build on.

I can't stress enough how important it is for you to get your site dialed in. Make sure that what you're doing works for the traffic that is already coming to you.

I often hear dealers talk about getting more traffic like it's the exact solution they need to succeed online. But the traffic is only as good as what you lead it to.

All the traffic in the world won't make a difference otherwise.

That's why we spent Chapter 7 talking about how to build a valuable web presence by creating incredible content.

So What's the Best Way to Drive Traffic?

I get asked this question all the time, and the answer is probably not what you're expecting.

There are currently two ways of driving traffic and, well... they are both the best way to drive traffic.

Organic and Paid traffic are always compared to one another, but the truth is that they both have their benefits and drawbacks.

I know that there are a lot of vendors out there who do one or the other, and both have their arguments against each other.

But the fact of the matter is that each play a role in your online marketing and need to work in harmony with one another to get the best results. More on this in a bit...

Health Nut Approved: Organic Traffic is the Healthy Long-term Choice

Organic search traffic is the best way to build trust and credibility. When your valuable content ranks high in search engines, people perceive you as the leader.

Getting your content or website to rank is where search engine optimization comes into the mix. Without it, your site has little-to-no ability to rank in search engines.

SEO is crucial to thriving online. It isn't something that you should cheap out on. As much as you might not want to hear that, whether you pay someone else to do it, or you do it yourself, there is an investment needed on your part.

Don't look for the cheapest alternative either. There are physical man hours needed to do SEO the right way.

When the cheap $99 - 500 dollar SEO gurus come knocking, I suggest you put on a pair of sneakers **(maybe the Skechers Tone-ups)** and start running as fast as you can!

But when SEO is done the right way, you will have a long-term sustainable online presence.

Think about the conversion path that we walked through in chapter 7. At each point of value along the way, you are engaging in an organic traffic strategy.

Each page of valuable content that you create will get ranked and indexed by search engines. Multiply that by each market segment, and you have a ton of content that will drive organic search traffic.

And again, the beauty of this is that your competition isn't doing it (and if they are, not very well)!

When Grant Cardone uttered the words, *"Content isn't king... Eyes are king!"* I wanted to smack his mouth. That one statement turned everything I believed on its head.

I had to sit there and let it process. After a few minutes, I understood the context of what he was saying.

You need to be visible if you want to get the attention of qualified buyers. People need to see you before they can consume the valuable content that you've spent so much time creating.

Of course, that will already be happening when you leverage existing traffic. But once that's dialed in, you need to flip the switch and get more. And since everything is in place, you'll be ready for more!

Getting in front of qualified buyers quickly is perhaps the largest drawback of an organic search strategy. It takes time and won't fill your immediate need for more traffic or leads.

On top of that, depending on what keywords you want your site to rank for, it could take months (and sometimes years) to achieve success.

Don't let that scare you, though. Without an organic search strategy in place, you won't have a foundation strong enough to do anything else online.

Organic traffic is a long-term, sustainable approach to traffic generation online. If you want to live a long life online, focus on implementing an organic traffic strategy asap!

Release the Floodgates with Paid Traffic

Have you ever seen the floodgates open on a dam before? In an instant, millions of gallons of water

pour out of the floodgates with incredible force.

But when the floodgates close, the water (with all its force) stops. What was there in massive quantities, ends in an instant.

That's the best way I could think of to describe paid traffic. It's powerful because when you want it, you can flip the switch and watch traffic pour into your site immediately.

But when you stop paying for it, the virtual floodgates close and the traffic stops as quickly as it came.

The fact that you can get immediate traffic is a massive benefit, though. Especially if you have an incredible offer that you need to get instant eyes on.

And when you have a conversion path (and valuable content) in place, the effectiveness of your paid search is even more powerful.

Here's why:

With paid search, you don't open just any floodgates. You open extremely targeted floodgates. The only ones that open are the ones that will release the specific audience that you want.

And instead of just pouring that audience into a generic pool, you can lead them exactly where they need to go to your site.

That means that you can target and attract buyers who are at specific phases of your conversion path.

Using the example from chapter 7, here's what I mean.

Let's say that you want to target young families who already know that they need a Minivan. Instead of leading them to your "Reasons Why…" page, you can lead them to the Minivan comparison page instead.

After all, they already believe that they need a MiniVan and are now much more likely to be comparing which make/model is the best for them.

The great thing about this approach to paid traffic is that it doesn't matter what ad platform you use. The goal, whether you're using Google, Facebook or Twitter ads, is to lead targeted consumers to a relevant page on your site.

I can't tell you how many dealer paid search campaigns are doing the opposite. It's shocking! They spend a ton of money on ads that, no matter what, lead consumers to the homepage of their website.

This was the case for a dealer's Google Adwords account that I audited. They were spending thousands of dollars on pay-per-click ads each month. Sure they were driving a ton of traffic, but their metrics was awful.

When I took a deeper look, I noticed that no matter what PPC ad I clicked on, they all led to the mobile homepage of this dealer's website.

Ugh! Think of the damage that this is doing...

When you drive paid traffic the right way, you can attract targeted buyers to content on your website that is specifically designed for them. Following this pattern, your organic and paid traffic strategies work in harmony.

Here's where things get even more powerful. Are you ready?

Using Google or Facebook's ads platform, you can install something on your website called a "pixel."

This pixel is a piece of code that's used to keep track visitors when they land on specific pages on your website. You can use this information to gain powerful insights into the interests of those visiting your site.

Once you know their interests, you can retarget them online wherever they go as long as ads are permitted on the page.

This happens to me all the time. I visit a website, pick up the pixel, and like magic start seeing ads on Facebook that are relevant to the site I was just visiting.

Here's an example of how it might work for you:

Let's say you have a paid traffic campaign that drives consumers to your vehicle comparison page. The goal of that page is to get people to click-through to your in-stock inventory page.

You can install a pixel on the in-stock inventory page and deliver relevant ads about that make/model only to people that have visited that page.

Doing so will keep that make/model at the forefront of the consumer's mind because it will follow them around the web via ads. In this way, we can hyper-target customers with messages after they have shown interest.

Can you see how both methods of traffic generation have their ups and downs?

On the one hand, organic traffic is slower but much more sustainable. On the other hand, paid search is hyper-targeted, immediate but will also stop when you close your wallet.

The ideal online traffic strategy should include both organic and paid methods. When you follow the pattern outlined in chapter 7 and 8, there's only one thing left for you to do.

Measure.

CHAPTER EIGHT QUESTIONS

Who has traffic problems?

What are the two main ways of driving traffic to your website?

What are the benefits and drawbacks of each traffic source?

DON'T WAIT, **DOMINATE!**

RELY ON THE DATA,
NOT YOUR GUT

Have you ever heard someone say that they made a decision based on what their gut was telling them? Early on in my online marketing adventures, I learned a valuable lesson about gut decisions.

My gut sucks at making decisions. I'm not kidding! But guess what, yours does too! Sorry to break that to you.

I hear people ask all the time, **"What's your gut telling you?"** as if it's going to help me make better, or more profitable decisions. Has this ever happen to you?

Some of the best advice I can offer you is that you should tell your gut to **'shut up'** and mind its own business. At least until you've given yourself enough time to gather data.

Here's the thing: most gut decisions are still the result of gathering data. The difference between good or bad gut decisions is the level of data that they were based on. **PERIOD.**

Let me explain.

Think about the last pair of shoes you bought. You probably made a decision on which ones to buy after you tried a bunch on.

You determined which ones were most comfortable, or which ones you liked the

113

look of. After gathering and analyzing the data, you made a decision.

I'm no psychic, but does that sound about right?

It doesn't matter what business you're in, most people never gather or analyze enough data to make profitable decisions.

This is especially true when it comes to online marketing, which is a shame.

Data Doesn't Lie

We have more abundant access to data now than ever before in the history of the planet, yet people are still making 'gut decisions'.

Everything online can be tracked, measured and analyzed. We can pinpoint the phase of the buying process consumers are in, where they came from and what they did when they were on your site.

Yet, some of you are still making **'gut decisions'.**

We can follow people on the web based on their search behavior and what content they consume.

Yet, some of you are still making **'gut decisions'.**

But it doesn't have to be this way. You can make profitable marketing decisions and thrive online using data as your guide.

You can do this because the data doesn't lie. It won't sugar coat anything for you. With data, you get the plain-Jane, stone cold truth about your online performance.

Data is only as good as the intended result

In the automotive industry, we are notorious for only tracking certain metrics. Site traffic, conversion (leads), units sold, time on site or bounce rate (just to name a few).

The problem is that, for the most part, metrics are often looked at from a high level. They are rarely analyzed with the intended marketing goal(s) in mind.

When you view your data out of context, it will always look bad.

I was consulting a dealership who was in need of severe organic traffic repair. They weren't ranking for several crucial search terms online. They were getting crushed by the competition as far as visibility goes.

I suggested a plan of action that would help repair their organic search rankings and help them gain more visibility in Google.

Within a month, their site's organic ranking began to improve by leaps and bounds.

There was only one problem...

They didn't view the increase in organic traffic as a success. Somewhere in the back of their minds, they weren't concerned with repairing and increasing organic traffic.

They just wanted more leads.

It didn't matter how many increases the data showed. All they cared about was an increase in leads, and that was the metric they were using to measure success. The data can either look good or bad depending on how you align it with your intended marketing goals.

You're probably wondering why this dealer couldn't achieve several marketing goals at once? I completely understand! I mean, why can't they repair their organic ranking and get more leads at the same time?

Online marketing is a process, **not an event.**

If you want to get the most out of your online marketing efforts, it's crucial to make updates and then review what's working or not.

It's much easier to do this when your focus is on a single set of goals. You will be less overwhelmed and get much more done in the long run.

I'm not saying that you can't kill two birds with one stone. If you do any of what we're talking about properly, that will naturally happen.

I am suggesting that if you want to understand how data affects decisions, start with one goal, one campaign and track it.

Data is not one size fits all

Nobody can tell you what to expect from your online marketing until they know the specifics of your current online situation.

I think it's funny when I attend conferences and experience a whole room of dealers get worried about their data. Some narrow-minded speaker or vendor has provided information that comes from a single dimension.

They speak in ideal terms, and never consider the online situation of each dealer in the room.

After the conference, the uproar begins. Dealers begin calling their vendors and demanding that things get done the way they learned it at the conference.

They return to work convinced at how every dealer in the nation should be performing.

If that isn't backward thinking, then I don't know what is. I mean, we've spent much of this book talking about separating yourself from the competition, not becoming exactly like them!

The best way to improve online and get better results is to compare yourself and your data to, well...you!

Think about it. You would never compare yourself to a bodybuilder or fitness expert when you've just started working out, would you?

Even though you might have a recipe to follow that will help you get in shape, you are unique. From your metabolism to how your body absorbs nutrition, you can only compare your progress to you.

Your dealership is unique. You need to be thinking about progress in terms that make sense for you, and then create plans that help you achieve success.

Now let's say that getting more leads is the only metric you care about. It's in your best interest to use the leads from the previous month as a benchmark.

And instead of doing the same thing and hoping for different results, you need to create a plan that will help increase the leads next month.

You also need to be mindful of other factors that affect the amount of leads you receive.

For example, at certain times of the years, leads typically drop in number. That's important to note so that you don't think things are falling apart, panic and revert to the old way of doing things.

Keeping track of consumer trends will help you create reasonable benchmarks at different times during the year.

Data that Most Vendors Don't Want You To See

Most of the time when dealers sign into Google Analytics, they never go past the first dashboard.

They look at the average time on site, bounce rate, sessions, and visitors. From those metrics, they believe they are getting the gist of what they need to know...

But Google Analytics is an incredibly powerful and robust tool that you need to understand for a variety of reasons.

First, when you have access to Google Analytics, it's much more difficult to get fake data. It adds a layer of transparency to the relationship you have with your vendors and empowers you to hold them accountable.

Second, you'll gain access to metrics that most vendors wouldn't show you otherwise. Metrics that will give you a deeper understanding of where to improve or what to duplicate.

Here are four powerful reports that will help you do this:

1. CHANNELS REPORT:

The Channel Report will give you a deeper understanding of the most common traffic sources that lead people to your site. From organic and paid traffic to referral and social traffic, we use this report on a daily basis.

It makes a huge difference knowing how people are finding you. Especially if you're running specific marketing campaigns and want to know if they're working.

Imagine being able to tell if your social media posts are driving traffic to your site. The channels report will keep you in the loop!

2. SITE CONTENT REPORT:

Once the traffic lands on your website, the Site Content Report will show you what pages consumers interact with.

This report will show you whether the content you've created is well received or not. From here, you can either make plans to improve low performing pages or enhance the pages that are already working well.

Using the site content report, nothing gets left to guesswork. You won't need to waste time figuring out if your content is relevant. This report will give you the goods.

3. SEARCH ENGINE OPTIMIZATION QUERIES REPORT:

I think of this report as a digital crystal ball. When you study it, you will find out what consumers are searching for and how they found you. When you get the hang of it, this report will make you a wizard.

On top of that, you'll also be able to see where your site ranks in a search engine and how often consumers choose you.

Can you imagine how powerful knowing this information will make you?

You can use this data to identify growth opportunities in your market. You'll be able to see who is outranking you, and with some research, determine why.

4.INTEGRATED ADWORDS DATA:

Okay, so this isn't a single report, but integrating your Google Adwords data directly into Google Adwords is a must if you're doing any level of digital advertising.

Doing so will help you gain valuable insights into how your digital ads are performing and aligning with your marketing objectives.

Once your Google Analytics and Google Adwords accounts are linked, you'll start gathering valuable insights into consumer behavior and allow you to see their activities while on your site.

Are you connected?

Do you have access to your Google Analytics account or is it being held hostage by your website provider?

Don't settle for the metrics that are provided through the platforms you use. If you want to see how your website is performing, you need the REAL Google Analytics access.

I can't stress how important it is for you to have access (or control) of your data so that you can use it to take your online business to the next level.

Let your competition continue down the path of gut decisions and guesswork. Where you're headed, you won't have time for that nonsense.

Using data as your guide, you're positioned to advance and conquer the market.

CHAPTER NINE QUESTIONS

What's the best way to make online marketing decisions?

What is the Channels Report?

What is the Search Engine Optimization Queries Report?

Why is connecting your Adwords and Analytics account beneficial?

CONCLUSION
WHERE RUBBER MEETS THE ROAD

DON'T WAIT, **DOMINATE!**

124

DON'T WAIT, **DOMINATE!**

DON'T JUST PLAN TO TAKE ACTION. DO IT!

Alright, it's time to face the facts.

How much advice have you received but still lack results?

How many conferences or webinars have you attended and still don't feel like you have what you need to succeed?

I hear this all the time, and it's a shame. With such abundant access to information, everyone should be achieving their definition of success.

The truth is that I've given you everything that I do that works for me and thousands of other dealerships worldwide.

You've gained access to the most powerful and proven online marketing concepts out there. They work in every industry, including (ESPECIALLY) automotive.

You're armed with the information, tools and resources needed to succeed online. We've looked through some examples and exercises together. You've learned the recipe and the ingredients in it. Now what?

Have you ever considered what's separating the knowledge you've acquired from the results you expect? There are many schools of thought on this topic, but in my experience, I've narrowed it down.

It's not enough to just keep listening to the theories and strategies out there. It's not enough to keep attending conferences or attending webinars.

All the notes you've taken, meetings you've had with your team and dollars that you've spent are all worthless unless...

You eventually do something with the information that you have.

Most people like the thought of achieving results. They like to feel hopeful and motivated. That's likely how you've felt as you've read this book.

Don't get me wrong. I'm not saying that hope and motivation don't play a role in your success. But don't mistake those feelings for actual success.

Have you ever heard the saying, *"Knowledge is power"*?

I've heard it used so often, and I used to agree wholeheartedly with it. But then I learned something valuable. Something that changed the course of my entire life and career. Something that certainly had a positive effect in my online marketing ventures...

Knowledge isn't power until you know what to do with it.

You see, the only thing that separates strategy from success is action. You must put your knowledge to use! The information in this book is useless if you don't take action on it.

That goes for any knowledge that you acquire in life. If you don't take action on it, it does you no good!

We talk a lot about how much theory there is in the automotive industry. But at the end of the day, **application** and **execution** is what you need to thrive!

Why are so many dealers merely surviving online, then? If action is all that's needed, what's the big deal?

Truth be told, most people give themselves more reasons NOT to take action than to take it. In fact, that's the exact reason most of your competitors will never do anything I talk about in this book.

When I first decided to take control of my company's destiny, it was frightening. I had a lot of people telling me to wait and become better prepared to do the big things that I wanted to do.

Like many people, I could have used those excuses to hold me back from achieving greatness. I'd be looking back with regrets right now.

I'm so glad I didn't, though. I'm glad that I decided to not let anything get in my way. I had the knowledge and was dying to put it into application.

The results speak for themselves.

I understand why dealers are hesitant to put this information into application, though.

It sounds different than anything they've ever learned before. Because of that, they retreat. They think it sounds risky or not accurate.

But just because you haven't heard of something before, **doesn't mean it's not right**.

When I first became exposed to these online marketing concepts, some of them made logical sense. Others caused me to stretch.

You need to ask yourself one very important question...

Why would you be okay doing the same thing as everyone else but hope for different results? Isn't that definition of insanity?

The reason dealers are having such a hard time differentiating right now is because everyone is doing the same thing. Then they complain that nothing is working. And then they blame it on their web provider. #insidejoke.

As I said, this stuff works for every industry including automotive.

As I've worked with dealers throughout the world, I've observed a common theme. They like to wait and see who else is doing it first. Somehow that thought process minimizes the potential risks of failure.

But that is **the problem...**

Everyone is failing right now. The only way to go is up. Taking risks is a big part of succeeding in business.

But since these strategies have already been proven, there shouldn't be much hesitancy on your part. All the proof out there has absorbed the risk of failure.

The spirit of **Don't Wait, DOMINATE!** is taking action. Remember, while others are busy assessing the risk of what it will take to be successful, you have a serious competitive advantage. You can take actions today that they're not willing to!

People who wait around making sure that all their *'ducks are in a row'* often get left in the dust by those who take off running.

You need to be that person who takes off running. You need to take advantage of the fact that your competitors are clueless. You need to let them continue chasing one another while you silently slip out of sight and on to massive success online.

Don't wait to find out what they're doing. That is in no way a sign of what's working. In many ways, it's the validation of motion without movement.

Even worse than that are people who know everything there is to know about online marketing yet do nothing with it. As I said, knowledge isn't power until you know what to do with it.

There are enough walking encyclopedias for ten lifetimes in the automotive industry. We need more doers!

Look, I completely understand how it feels to want everything to be perfect before you take action. There is a certain comfort that comes from knowing you've minimized the risk of failure.

Your job might be on the line, and you need a massive win to solidify your position. You don't want to screw up just trusting someone else' words.

But I submit that you are at a greater risk of failure by failing to act. For every day that goes by without massive action on your part, you are narrowing the gap between you and your competition.

I also understand what it feels like to have all of this knowledge and not know where or how to get started. For many, that can be an overwhelming feeling. So overwhelming that they use it as an excuse to never do anything.

If that's how you feel, this is your turning point. When it comes to online marketing, if execution hasn't been a habit of yours, here is a simple step process to get started and achieve results.

1. Get yourself a notebook or task manager

This will serve as your to-do list for all of your online projects.

Start by defining your marketing goal. Think of where you'd like to end up. That way you'll be able to identify the steps needed to get you there.

Next, write down all the actions needed to get you from here to there. When you think of new actions, return to your list and add them.

129

Once you've completed a task, cross it off. Following this pattern will help you focus on the next action to take. Just stay focused on completing the next action, one task at a time.

When you make a habit of defining a goal and then writing the tasks to its achievement, success happens at lightning speed.

Don't give yourself the false perception that this will be immediate. Just because I say "lightning speed" doesn't mean that you can do nothing today and expect results tomorrow.

Don't think that this is going to be harder than it sounds, either. That's just another excuse that we come up with to get out of taking action. Most people think that way, and it's lame.

And so what if the path to success is harder than it sounds. If it leads to success, don't you want to be successful?

Big success is the result of taking many smaller steps. When you add all the steps up, they equal a completed goal. Don't be afraid, just start taking them!

That's it. I said I'd give you a simple "step" process to taking action, and that's it.

Identify your goal. Write down the steps that will get you there. **Take action.**

Wait...Was it Plan to Take Action or Take Action to Plan?

What? Wait a minute… shouldn't planning come before you take action?

Well, yes and no. Let me explain…

Taking the time to sit down and plan your online marketing efforts in and of itself is taking action.

But I wanted to make sure you understood how crucial your

actions would be to achieving online success first. Especially because too much of the wrong planning can get in the way of taking future action.

There are examples of this all over the place. Everyone that's had a big idea at some point or another has gone so overboard with their plan that they failed to execute.

I can't tell you how many white boards I've filled with grandiose plans that have never made it into implementation.

That's why most successful businesses today started with a plan on the back of a napkin. It sounds so cliché because of it's simplicity, but simple plans are the ones that get implemented.

I figured this out after enough frustration. The best way to get results is to break your marketing goals down to their simplest form.

Keep your plans simple and focused. Plan and chart out actions for a single initiative at a time.

For example, if your goal is to increase engagement on your Facebook posts, it's better to break that down into bite-size chunks.

Here are some questions you can ask that will help you do this. Write your answers down in your notebook or task manager:

1. What is the main goal? Likes, comments or shares?
2. Who are these posts going to be for?
3. What topics are those people interested in?
4. When/how often will I post?
5. Are there better times of day to post? If so, when?
6. Who will create/write the posts? What's the deadline?

When you've finished answering those questions, you have the foundation of a plan. The clearer your understanding of the plan, the more power you have to execute when the time comes.

You've heard the saying, "When you fail to plan, you plan to fail"? Have you ever found an instance where that wasn't true?

There is no compensation for failing to plan. Here's why:

Without a plan, **you have no direction.**

When dealerships lack a digital marketing plan, it's obvious. Nobody knows what direction they should be going. They don't know what they want to achieve, so they all same the same thing: **"More leads!"**

Don't wait for your vendors to give you the direction, either. It doesn't work that way. Somewhere, somehow the perception has become that dealers pay vendors to know what the plan should be.

But none of that makes any sense without direction from you. It's your business. You can't have others tell you what your business is supposed to achieve. You need to have an idea and then hire them to do the work that will make it happen. They can bring it to life with proven strategies once they know what you want to have happen.

If not, they will never do the job that you think they should be doing for the money you give them.

Without a direction, you can't have goals. If you don't have goals, everything up to this point in the book is garbage.

Your perception will always be that you're under-performing, and your analytics will always look bad.

Without a plan, you'll waste time and money

And what company wants to waste time and money?

You'll waste time because nobody will know what they should be doing. Everyone will be running around like chickens with their heads cut off.

Frustration levels will increase, and everyone will burst!

You'll waste money because the services and tools that you pay for will get ignored.

As a result, you or those that work with you will engage in random sporadic actions. Lots of motion, but no movement.

And when things stop going according to plan, what plan is it exactly?

Make sense?

If all you take are random actions, all you can expect are random results.

Take a Deep Breath and Enhance your Vision

As a kid, I remember hearing stories about my Grandfather's work ethic. Nearing retirement he was a custodian for a government corporation.

At the beginning of his shift, instead of rushing to get his tasks done, he would sit and think about them. In his mind, he would identify the best way to complete each task walking through each from start to finish in his mind.

When it came time to take action, he was so well prepared that he'd usually finish the job early and more efficiently than his co-workers. They could never figure out what his secret strategy was.

It was planning and action.

Planning and Action? That's all you have? That sounds too simple!

Don't you feel like sometimes we just hope things will be more difficult than they really are? It's almost as if we think that if it's difficult, the outcome will be better deserved?

133

I look back to the version of myself that was struggling to pull my company out of obscurity and chuckle a little.

I thought for sure that achieving my goal was going to be more difficult than it was.

For a short while, I used that as an excuse to not do the things that I wanted.

I eventually found out that when you combine a strategic plan with the right level of action, magic happens.

It's called, **Total Control.**

CHAPTER TEN QUESTIONS

What is your online marketing goal(s)?

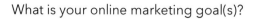

List the steps that you need to take in order
to achieve that goal.

List the people on your team needed to achieve your goal.

THIS IS THE END.

Hold on a minute here...

Are you still reading?

But I've just given you everything I have to offer on this topic.

...you still feel like there could be more, don't you? :)

Here's the cold hard truth behind *Don't Wait, DOMINATE!* - It's simple, but complex at the same time. That's not to suggest that you don't have the intellectual capacity to put this into action.

It doesn't just require you to know the recipe and each of the ingredients, it requires you to get cracking.

And like we've already talked about, that's often where most people get stuck.

Whatever you do, **don't stop here!**

Like I said, you're already armed with more information than all your competitors combined when it comes to doing online marketing the RIGHT way.

But unless you put these concepts into practice they'll just waste away on the shelf.

The fact is, the concepts of *Don't Wait, DOMINATE!* are hard to explain in print alone. That's why I'd like to invite you to my personal website: http://michaelacirillo.com/dominate where I will be posting complete walk-throughs of the concepts discussed in the book.

When you subscribe, you'll also gain access to my exclusive mastermind group where I will reveal the latest, cutting-edge strategies that will take you to the next level of success – FAST.

This group is also a great place for you to share what's working so that the members of the group can benefit from one another.

So here's a recap of what we've talked about to get you started:

1. Recognize that you already have everything you need to be successful online. Stop looking for some other magic system.

2. The market is cluttered...with crappy marketing. That's your most valuable resource, and you can start doing things differently, starting now.

3. This will work for your dealership because it works in every industry!

4. That's because online marketing success is a recipe. Here are the ingredients:

5. Knowing that every consumer has a different taste. There are RIGHT customers, and WRONG customers depending on the message you have.

6. When you segment the market, it enhances your ability to find the right customer. It also means that every WRONG customer is the RIGHT customer for something else you offer.

7. When you over deliver on value, your authority and credibility go through the roof. You'll do this by creating consistent and valuable content based on the topics that each market segment has an interest in.

8. You don't have a traffic problem.

9. 100% always rely on what the data is telling you. Your gut sucks at making decisions.

10. Get moving. Don't let the motions get in the way of your movement. Take the time you need to create a plan and then take action like a crazy beast!

There you have it. That's it!

Congratulations!

You now have an online marketing asset that will serve as a solid foundation. From here you can build whatever you want.

This will help you release the floodgates of online opportunity and THRIVE online...

There's only one thing left to do.

DON'T WAIT.
DOMINATE!

THANK YOU

There are many people who I'd to express sincere appreciation for. They have either directly or indirectly contributed to the adventure of writing this book.

My wife, **Kara** (*a.k.a. "Gorg"*) is my greatest cheerleader. She is my best friend. She comforts me, energizes me and empowers me to act beyond my own innate abilities. Her unwavering friendship, support and encouragement make my life rich. Together we will dominate life!

Dallin, **Tristan** and **Aria** are the reason why I get out of bed in the morning. I hope they know how much I love them and want them to succeed in life.

My parents, **Giuseppe and Maria Cirillo**, deserve more credit than I can give. They have sacrificed so much to make sure that I was positioned for greatness. They taught me to love God and what it means to be a man. The only way I can repay them is to pass what they've taught me onto my children.

Thanks, **Joshua Sprague**, for coaching me through the process of writing a book. Every day for the last 3 years, my calendar has reminded me to work on my book. It's been a goal of mine for such a long time. Joshua's resources and coaching have helped this become a reality.

Thank you to my team. You are a group of powerful individuals and together we will revolutionize an entire industry.

Thank you, **Robert Wiesman** and **Jason Prud'homme** for contributing ideas and helping me flesh out my thought processes. You've been listening to me talk about "THE BOOK" for quite some time, and without your help, this might not have seen the light of day. In addition, **Colin Burke** is to thank for this book cover looking incredible. He was able to take my vision and make it look freaking awesome.

Tracy Myers is someone who I've considered a mentor for quite a few years now. From the first time I met him in person, I thirsted for his knowledge and wisdom. Although it may have come off as obnoxious, he never once made me wrong and always encouraged me. Today I'm glad for our friendship and his help in reviewing and endorsing this book.

According to **David Bradley**, I "Yoda mind-hacked" him into reading this book. Even with an air tight schedule, he found the time to dig in and provide feedback and encouragement. If that isn't sincere friendship, I don't know what is. Thank you.

I respect what **JD Rucker** has to say. I have followed his work for quite a few years and knew I needed his feedback on the manuscript. Thank you for taking the time and for your friendship. I appreciate it very much.

Glenn Pasch was an invaluable resource for me on this project. I was fortunate enough to sit with him in person and review his notes and suggestions. He has been a great support and I am grateful to call him a friend.

I'm grateful to my friend, **Marcus Sheridan** for providing valuable feedback on this project. Even with an extremely busy work/travel schedule, he was able to find the time to review this book and share his thoughts. Thank you.

Finally, thanks are in order for you, **my readers**. Getting this information into your hands was a great motivator for me. You and I belong to the greatest industry on planet earth. Your feedback, whether through the podcast, social media or email has been an invaluable source of strength for me. Thank you for your support.

WHO IS
MICHAEL CIRILLO

Michael Cirillo is a dad who doubles as a businessman, an entrepreneur who loves the hustle; a Dreamer who creates reality , and a lifelong student.

His digital marketing and consulting agency, **FlexDealer**, works with dealerships and small/medium businesses around the world to develop digital strategies, websites and content. Michael has been serving the automotive industry specifically since 1998.

Michael is also the Cohost of **The Dealer Playbook Podcast**, which features weekly conversations with other elite marketers such as Jay Baer, Gary Vaynerchuk, Marcus Sheridan, Grant Cardone, Dan Waldschmidt, Tracy Myers and many more - free for today's automotive professionals.

To date, his podcast is listened to by thousands of automotive professionals in over 50 countries worldwide.

Michael lives in Vernon, British Columbia, Canada with his wife and three children.

Connect with Michael:

mc@michaelacirillo.com
Twitter: @MichaelACirillo

NOTES

12   1   Three Automotive Digital Marketing Tips. Download it here: http://www.flexdealer.com/automotive-digital-marketing-tips

12   2   Perhaps it still does...

14   3   http://www.prnewswire.com/news-releases/nada-chairman-new-car-dealers-are-catalysts-for-change-300025213.html

29   4   NADA Report: Approx. 16,200 franchise new-car dealerships with both domestic and international franchises. CADA Report: Approx. 3,200 franchise new-car dealerships as of January 2015. Mexico not included.

30   5   TIME Magazine Article, "The Internet's Big Bang" http://content.time.com/time/specials/packages/article/0,28804,1902809_1902810_1905184,00.html

36   6   Dasha/Petrenko/shutterstock.com survey of 1000 US adults who bought a vehicle in the past 12 months.

43   7   The surprising facts about who shops online and on mobile: http://www.businessinsider.com/the-surprising-demographics-of-who-shops-online-and-on-mobile-2014-6

43   8   Online retail sales to hit $34-billion in Canada by 2018: - http://business.financialpost.com/news/retail-marketing/online-retail-sales-to-hit-40-billion-in-canada-by-2018

67   9   The DPB Podcast #50 w/ Jay Baer: http://www.thedealerplaybook.com/50

79   10   How to Win Friends and Influence People, written by Dale

DON'T WAIT, **DOMINATE!**

79 11   Search Engine Land Article, "Google Still Doing At Least 1 Trillion Searches Per Year": http://www.searchengineland.com/google-1-trillion-searches-per-year-212940

90 12   Digital Drives Auto Shopping: 82% of purchasers are in-market for three months or less. Source: Millward Brown Digital/Google Vehicle Shopper Path to Purchase Study

94 13   When dealers or vendors plop random low value offers all over their site thinking that consumers will oblige. That's just the name I've given it... :)

103 14   According to http://www.internetlivestats.com/internet-users/

113 That may or may not be an image of my likeness...

DON'T WAIT, **DOMINATE**

DON'T WAIT, **DOMINATE!**

Manufactured by Amazon.ca
Bolton, ON

11107732R00083